"Interviewing is all about selling, so what makes more sense than asking an innovative expert in sales how to ace your interview? She gets to the point quickly with easy-to-read, practical advice so you can nail the interview and settle into your new job. A must-have for any job seeker."

—Aricia LaFrance, PhD, therapist, career coach, and author of *Unlocking the Secrets of the Successful Career Seeker*

"You've won an interview for that job you really want. Way to go! But before the interview read *Hired!* by Elinor Stutz. Her concrete, practical, and winning advice will show you how to present the "uniquely you" applicant that they are desperately seeking. Read it, take her advice, and get hired!"

—Loral Langemeier, CEO and founder of Live Out Loud, Inc., and best-selling author of the Millionaire Maker series and *Put More Cash in Your Pocket*

"Learn from a top sales pro how to sell your most valuable asset: yourself. Elinor Stutz tackles the hiring process with wit, integrity, and creativity, sharing the insider's secrets she's used over a successful career to win new business and nab promotions. Get *Hired!* and get hired!"

—Gail Z. Martin, author of *30 Days to Social Media Success*

"I highly recommend reading *Hired!* if you are determined to find a great job. The sales approach to finding a job really makes sense to me but I've never applied it in the past. Then I read Elinor's book and applied a number of Elinor's recommendations. I had several offers to choose from and found the perfect job for me."

—Jackie M., hedge fund CFO

"Using sales strategies, Elinor Stutz shows readers how to sell themselves and seal the deal during a job interview. Her techniques are entirely unique and they really work!"

—Randy Peyser, author of *The Power of Miracle Thinking*

"I love Elinor for lots of reasons: She's got tons of heart, her advice is always practical, and her techniques work. She taught this nice girl how to get the sale and she'll teach you how to get hired!"

—Tara Rodden Robinson, PhD, "The Productivity Maven," co-leader of the business development and marketing special interest group for the International Association of Coaching

"You're convinced that no one will ever hire you so you're just walking down the street of life, kicking road apples. I know how you feel and so does Elinor Stutz, who wrote the excellent book you hold in your hands. Hold on tight, because this book can turn your life around. She'll teach you how to maximize your natural assets and how to attractively present them to the best job prospects available. In short, she's going to help you hear those magic words, "You're hired."

—Hank Trisler, author of *No Bull Selling*

"This is the premiere book on how to get hired! Use Elinor's time-tested and proven techniques to get the job you want. A must-read for this new economy."

—Jill Lublin, international speaker and best-selling author of *Guerilla Publicity*, *Networking Magic*, and *Get Noticed, Get Referrals*

"I just picked up Elinor's *Hired!* and wasn't able to put it down! Her stories captured me and I felt I was right there with her, learning alongside her and feeling very inspired and uplifted. *Hired!* offers great information which can be applied in any area of our lives and will greatly improve all relationships. I highly recommend you get a copy for yourself and all your friends."

—Tina van Leuven, PhD, Innerdelight.com

"JOBS, JOBS, JOBS—it is all that matters. Elinor has jumped years into the future where everyone is hired…. As chairman of the largest small business trade organization in the world and a best-selling author, [and] coaching such superstars as Tony Robbins, Jack Canfield, John Gray, John Asrahraaf, Bob Proctor, Lisa Nichols, Les Brown, and more, [I recommend] *Hired!* to everyone…on our best-seller lists."

—Berny Dohrman, founder of CEO Space

"Stutz presents practical material on building relationships for success in business. Her real-world advice is loaded with common-sense ideas, and her stories will [keep] you hanging on her every word. She has a true command of sales strategies that succeed."

—Betty Louise, certified life coach and host of Green Think Internet Radio

Hired!

Hired!

How to Use Sales Techniques to Sell Yourself on Interviews

By Elinor Stutz

The Career Press, Inc.
Pompton Plains, N.J.

HIRED!
EDITED BY KIRSTEN DALLEY
TYPESET BY GINA HOOGERHYDE
Cover design by Rob Johnson/Toprotype
Printed in the U.S.A. by Courier

To order this title, please call toll-free 1-800-CAREER-1 (NJ and Can-ada: 201-848-0310) to order using VISA or MasterCard, or for further information on books from Career Press.

The Career Press, Inc.
220 West Parkway, Unit 12
Pompton Plains, NJ 07444
www.careerpress.com

Library of Congress Cataloging-in-Publication Data

Stutz, Elinor.
    Hired! : how to use sales techniques to sell yourself on inter-views / by Elinor Stutz.
            p. cm.
        Includes index.
        ISBN 978-1-60163-142-8 -- ISBN 978-1-60163-685-0 (eb-ook) 1. Employment interviewing. 2. Selling--Psychological aspects. 3. Career development. I. Title.

HF5549.5.I6S78 2011
650.14'4--dc22

2010025455

Dedication

*T*o my sales prospects and former managers, both of whom inspired me and provided me with the insight to share with my clients and readers of this book.

Acknowledgments

*D*uring my first year in sales, it was a battle between the men trying to force me out and me refusing to leave. I had no idea what to do on appointments because there was no training. Naturally I was curious about one thing: How could I get a better job? Whenever I was invited in for a new sales appointment, I questioned my prospects intensively about how they were able to secure their jobs despite all the competition during the economic downturn of the 1990s. Their collective advice was excellent and helped me interview better throughout my career. I also must mention the people in sales management who inspired me to brush up on and refine my interviewing skills on almost a yearly basis. Because of them, I now have much insight to share with you and the public at large.

I view myself as a messenger for what works. In order to provide you with a truly well-rounded perspective on interviewing, I asked experts in the field of career transition, marketing, and hiring to provide their input, too. For their insight, friendship, and contributions to this book, my deepest appreciation goes out to Ed Stutz, my husband of many years who wholeheartedly supports my entrepreneurial endeavors and provided excellent stories of his career; Netanya Stutz, our daughter and marketing communications guru; Jeff Stutz, our son, who keeps us abreast of the high-tech industry; Christine LeMay, career coach; Kristi Frlekin, branding expert; Rebecca Kieler, career consultant; Linda Stokely, career consultant; Don Cracraft, the "document control guy," for his continued support; and those who submitted their personal interviewing stories to share with you, my readers.

Special recognition must be given to Bethany Brown, whose editing talents helped make my first book, *Nice Girls DO Get the Sale: Relationship Building That Gets Results*, an international success. My deepest appreciation goes to Bethany for once again performing her editorial magic on my initial submission to Career Press.

And a special thank you to Randy Peyser, CEO of Author One Stop, who helped me find the perfect publisher not once, but twice. This time she strongly recommended John Willig as the perfect agent to put me in touch with Career Press.

We all know you should not judge a book by its cover, but when I first laid eyes on the cover design for this book, I jumped for joy! I proudly tell everyone that I now have both the yin and the yang of book covers.

And finally, a very big thank-you to the entire team at Career Press, not only for offering a contract, but also for recognizing this book's potential for helping, with a community-service mindset, those who have experienced long-term unemployment and those who wish to move their careers into fast-forward.

Contents

Prologue

*Y*ou are probably wondering if you really want to invest the time to read this book. What caught your attention and caused you to pick it up in the first place? Most likely there is something going on in your career that caused the title to speak to you. Perhaps you are bored where you are, or the opportunity you stayed for faded away. Perhaps you have new management who doesn't share your philosophy for conducting business. Perhaps the current environment just isn't friendly or casual enough. Or, perhaps you've been unemployed for a very long time and need to get back to work. Some of you may wish to move to a different part of the country, work closer to home, work shorter hours, or get paid more for your work. Maybe childcare is a requirement that isn't offered where you are.

Just as I asked you why you picked up this book, I ask every potential client I meet what caught their interest in me. Making a sale of any type—or in this case, getting a job—is all about becoming familiar with and understanding the needs of the other person or the company. When you approach your interview as if you were about to make a sale, you will have a far better chance at securing the job you truly want. Asking relevant questions starts the process off on the right foot. The entire process of securing a job actually *is* a sales cycle. Please read the Salesology section before you begin the rest of the book; it will help you understand each stage of the cycle in order to know how to apply it to the job search and interview process, so that you may quicken your journey to hearing that word "HIRED!"

Preface

As a teenager, I was told that all I had to do on an interview was sell myself. At the time, I had no idea what that meant. I certainly had no idea at the time how significant that directive would be for me throughout my career.

Later in life, I entered the corporate sales world after hearing my husband tell me that I had the personality of a salesperson. Believe it or not, I was horrified! In my mind I pictured the stereotypical, shady used car salesman using unethical means to get the sale. As my career took me from sales team to sales team at a variety of companies, I always got the job I wanted. In each job, I paid attention to what each team had in common and why we were chosen to become a part of that team, and I always became the top producer of each new team by the third or fourth month of employment.

I came to realize that no matter what you want in life, when you remain focused and determined to get that special something, the best way to get there is by following the selling process, better known as the sales cycle. As you interview, it's important to think of yourself as the commodity or "brand," and your interviewer as your "prospect." You must persuade that person to see you as the best candidate for the job and "buy" what you are "selling." If you sell yourself on the interview properly, you will turn your one special prospect into your client—the person who will tell you that you're HIRED!

When I was 16, I interviewed for the very first time for a part-time secretarial position. I heard my first objection when I was told, "You are the first person to come in for an interview so I'm not certain you will be the best fit. But just out of curiosity, when would you be able to get started?" Not recognizing the threat of competition or the possibility of not getting the job, I replied, "I cleared the afternoon for this interview. Would you like to test my ability now?" It was my innocence that came shining through and helped me secure the job.

Although I had never sold a thing up to that point, I learned years later this was a natural "close" that helped me make the "sale." It was a close because my offer to stay demonstrated my commitment as well as my ability to prevent others (pre-empting the competition) from coming in to interview for the job. I passed with flying colors and I was ultimately paid for those volunteered hours. The position

I applied for was the start of a fruitful relationship. One month prior to every holiday throughout my high school years, I called my boss and asked him if he would like me to work in his office. I always had a job waiting for me.

Since then, I have learned two important things that will help you to interview better. First, any time you express an opinion or make a request, you are selling. Most people fear the concept of selling and think it means being unethical or sleazy. In successful selling, the opposite is actually true. When you listen actively, ask intelligent questions, and try to understand the other person's needs and goals with a focus on solutions, you will be far better positioned to make the sale—and get the job. Second, you must have a very strong belief system in place that you will succeed. My two favorite quotes are, "If you believe you can, you will, and if you believe you can't, you won't" (Mark Twain), and "Failure is not an option" (Eleanor Roosevelt).

Throughout my career, I have either created a position for myself or have been offered the job I sought. People say that's because I'm a natural-born saleswoman. Only one instance comes to mind in which I did not get the job I wanted right away, which is testament to the fact that not all interviews will go well. I left that interview to get my initial experience elsewhere. Three years later, with some sales success behind me, I was much more confident in my abilities, so I decided to return to that same company that had rejected me. To my relief, the hiring manager I had met with previously had switched to another office, and I was able to secure a higher-ranking position than the previous one for which I was shown the door.

There are two things you can learn from this. First, when you do not qualify for a job, get the experience elsewhere. If a particular firm is your dream company, get the experience and go back for another interview down the road. In the big picture, this is only a detour in your career, and it might ultimately get you where you want to be. Second, you must be honest about whether or not your personality fits with the department and/or the manager you will be working with. If you can detect conflict during the interview and you are hired, your time at the company will very likely be short-lived. Speaking from experience, it is frustrating to keep looking for new jobs, and it does not sit well with interviewers when they realize you have had several. So my advice is always to be true to yourself and know what will work for you and what won't.

The goal of this book is to help you get the interviews you want, and make the most out of every interview you have. I recognize what works for some people may not work for others. As with any sales endeavor, you have to make the style and approach your own. Your unique capabilities must come through loud and clear. Marketing gurus call this your unique selling proposition. (Later in the book, I will refer to this as your brand.) You also need to know about marketing and entrepreneurship. Entrepreneurship involves the ambitious, creative side of selling, whereas marketing is the art and act of attracting others. Using your marketing knowledge and skills will help you communicate effectively and make you memorable. Your professionalism, as evidenced in how you present yourself and how you communicate, should be a major part of your personal brand. When you use these three principles—sales, entrepreneurship, and marketing— you have a much better chance of securing that job. And when these are combined with old-fashioned niceties and cutting-edge technology, you will create a winning combination designed to help you hear the word "HIRED!"

Salesology:
The Stages of the Sales Cycle

W hen I began my sales career, I was told that to be successful, I must follow the sales cycle in its proper order and pay close attention to the details in each stage. Of course, my next question (offered with a blank stare) was, "What is a sales cycle?" As we now know that interviewing follows the sales cycle, I have outlined here the very basics of what the cycle entails. As you read through this book, you will soon learn how to apply each stage of the sales cycle to successful interviewing.

Making a sale is a finite process that has a beginning and an end. The first stage, before you even get to meet with anyone, involves cultivating and maintaining a positive mindset, and the last stage involves you obtaining (hopefully) the first round of business—or that new job. The cycle continues as you develop additional sales or advance your career. To achieve these goals, the precise steps in between (as detailed in the forthcoming chapters) must be executed well and be based upon relationship-building.

Following are the basic stages of the sales cycle, with a description of how each stage applies to the job search process:

Mindset—reflection and moving forward: You will find it very difficult to sell anything, let alone get the job you want, unless you fully believe you will be successful. Understanding your history of past accomplishments as well as setbacks will help you plan better for the future. This kind of self-knowledge will increase your confidence and help you to achieve better results.

Goal-setting and planning: Salespeople are given goals for achieving quotas or bringing in a set amount of revenue for the year. These amounts are normally way above what anyone believes is realistic or possible. However, with careful planning, and adhering to that plan every single day, the real professionals are able to achieve their goals, and usually even surpass them. The same goes for you as you search for and land the job you want.

Sales funnel—playing the field: As possibilities for sales or jobs arise, you will soon learn which prospects are valid and which are not, turning some into qualified leads and pushing them deeper into the sales funnel. The prospects that make it all the way through the funnel are those who become your clients or potential new employers.

Brand development: Whether you are employed or not, first and foremost you are your own brand. Consistency and the ability to succinctly communicate what you are all about are essential for building trust, confidence, and likeability. These are all key ingredients for getting the sale—and the right job.

Prospecting: Once you know the basic profile for your ideal company, you set out to find as many prospects as possible that fit your description. This includes all of the possible methods for finding prospects, including going door-to-door, networking in person, and the use of social media.

Researching your prospects: Once you find appropriate prospects, you will want to research each one in as great a depth as time allows. Research is necessary for two reasons: one, for you to sound intelligent on the interview; and two, for you to know whether it is worthwhile to pursue the job. Your research is what establishes your credibility, from the phone introduction to the actual appointment.

Qualifying prospects: It would be a complete waste of time to apply to every job ever posted. Your thorough research will help you answer your pressing questions before you ever contact the prospect. For example, what is the company seeking in a candidate? Do you have the interest or the talent to do an excellent job? Is the industry in general doing well, and is the company profitable? These discerning questions will help you to qualify your prospects and to decide whether or not you should pursue them further.

Relationship selling: This is a relaxed, friendly style of selling that endeavors to find commonality with the other party. When you establish a good relationship early in the sales cycle or job search, you build confidence and trust in your abilities, and greatly increase the likelihood of getting the sale, or the job.

Overcoming objections: You will always encounter others' objections to doing business with you. This is when you apply your researched facts and showcase your talents in order to demonstrate how you will help the other person or company overcome their challenges. This differentiates you from your competition and serves to overcome any previous objections and put you in the lead for the sale (the job). Interviews are a two-way street. Just as you are trying to decide if this company is where you will be happy, the interviewing manager is trying to decide if you will be a team player who will be competent on the job. You will likely have difficult questions thrown at you to see how you handle the pressure, and it's your job to effectively field these questions and overcome any objections contained within them.

Trial close: Questions posed to determine if you are on track to get the sale are referred to as a trial close. If you briefly shared how you helped your past company to save money and then asked, "Is this the type of work dedication you are seeking?" this question would be considered a trial close.

Negotiation: Give and take is a part of every sale. Rarely will you receive everything you want. Therefore, when you negotiate your compensation, it is vital to know what you must have and what you are willing to forego in order to seal a deal that is satisfactory to all parties.

Final close: Most salespeople refer to the act of receiving business as closing. I prefer to think of getting the business as the start of a beautiful long-term relationship! Finally, your prospect has become your client, and your interviewing company has become your employer.

The sales cycle continues even after you get the job. Accomplished salespeople document and keep a record of their successes. You should do the same for your career advancement. Once you find a job, begin keeping a monthly one-page bulleted list noting all of your successes. This will help you sell yourself to management on your evaluations and when you are ready for a promotion.

Make sure you continue with your relationship-building, too. Make management your first priority when their requests come your way. Brainstorm challenges with them and keep them apprised of your projects and accomplishments. When you need additional help with a project or need to make a difficult request—for example, asking for a raise—your success rate will dramatically increase.

Clearly, getting to HIRED! is not the end of your selling. The sales cycle continuously repeats itself with everyone you meet throughout your career. To truly succeed, you need to build relationships with everyone around you and create a mutually beneficial support team.

Now let's get to the nitty-grittys of how to sell yourself on interviews!

Your Mindset

*C*ongratulations, you did it! You got the job interview! Your excitement is at an all-time high. But you are also getting more nervous by the second. Perhaps you haven't interviewed in a long time, or maybe you are lacking the necessary experience in some areas. Perhaps many people will be competing for the same job. The list of your concerns is continually growing. If that weren't enough, you now know you need to sell yourself on the interview, but you aren't certain how that's done. Are you getting nervous about the fact that you really need this job? Has your excitement begun to wear off just a bit? Are you focused on all of the bills that are piling up? Are the negative voices in your head beginning to dominate your thoughts? This is where you tell those voices and yourself to stop! This chapter will help calm your nerves and put your fears to rest. We will start putting together a plan of action to prepare mentally and verbally for your upcoming interview.

Analyze Your History and Change Your Future

Before you can move forward with a positive frame of mind, it would be helpful to gain perspective regarding your career history. What lessons can you learn from your past missteps and those of others? Which hard lessons will you avoid in the future? A retrospective before moving forward is called for. The following stories will remind you to reflect on your own situation and help you clarify what is important to you moving forward.

The company I was representing in 2001 became so bureaucratic that mixed messages were continually being sent to our sales force. It became mandatory to let management know upfront who your new and serious prospects were prior to continuing the sales process. I shared my list and was given my company's seal of approval. I will never forget the day I was about to secure business from a well-known company. My final step was to let my company know I would be picking up the client's deposit check to finalize the order that they previously approved. To my horror, I received word that my company no longer desired their business for a variety of reasons, and I was strongly advised to forego the appointment. Although I was certainly concerned (this was promising to be an enormous sale), I was more distressed knowing this was the third time my company turned down business I had found. It became clear that, once again, I needed to find another job. I thought that if I could just make it into high-tech—something I was craving—the rules for business would change into a more professional model. Many of my frustrations would disappear. I desperately wanted to enter into a new era of working hand-in-hand with my employer and having a positive impact on my clients. It would be far better than having the rules change at any given moment and fighting an old-world mentality.

An opportunity presented itself just in the nick of time. The job was described as selling advertising on financial Websites. I was new to the high-tech industry and had no idea how to do the job, but I was more than ready to give it a try. Anything would be better than remaining at the antiquated company that I represented at the time. The office remained steadfast in conducting business the way it always had, and showed no interest in adapting to new methods or even considering new ideas. Employees had little voice and were shown no appreciation. The only reason to show up for this job was the commission earned at the conclusion of a sale, but in my case this wasn't happening either.

Anything Is Not Better: Listen to Your Intuition

The hiring manager (we'll call him Bill) at the high-tech company and I met to discuss everything the job entailed. By that time I was adept at reading body language and facial expressions, so it became clear to me that there was an inconsistency between the Bill's vocabulary and his nonverbal communication. Therefore I did not trust him. What was most peculiar about our conversation was his lack of professionalism. We initially met at a coffee shop to discuss the details of the position. Of course, Bill was doing a sell job on me, explaining how the compensation package worked. Given the fact that this would be my first job in the high-tech industry, my main concern was whether there would be a "learning curve" that would allow me to reach my sales goals. Bill's answer to my question actually gave me the worst headache I had ever had. Rather than pull out documentation from his binder, he took a half-used napkin lying on the table to draw out how the goals and compensation plan would play out over the next 12 months. He expected me to make a decision about the job based on his sketches on a napkin that featured not only the compensation plan but also crumbs from his cookie. It was very telling.

At this point, there was no doubt whatsoever in my mind that Bill was lying, so I quickly picked up his napkin as he was about to throw it away. I wanted that napkin for safe-keeping. By this time, I was very in tune with reading people.

Remember, in any mode of communication, your words, actions, and deeds must be consistent and in alignment with each other. They are part of your brand. At any moment, no matter the circumstance, people will anticipate what they will get when they interact with you. The inconsistencies between Bill's words, facial expressions, and body language were red flags. The fact he did not bring an official compensation guide but instead chose to write the criteria out on a dirty napkin intended to be tossed told me that none of it was truthful. In fact, he looked worried when I reached for the napkin.

Weigh Your Must-Have List Against Taking a Calculated Risk

I had a raging headache for an entire week, knowing in my gut that I should not accept the job. On the other hand, I was making zero money back at the office, and the way things were going, there was no sense continuing to even show up there. Because of my lack of experience in the industry, this might be my only possibility for getting into the high-tech world. But I knew that doing so would entail great risk that I would be working for someone less than truthful and would have to find another job soon thereafter. The best I could hope for was to stay long enough to gain some experience. I was given only one week to make the decision of whether to accept or decline Bill's offer. Although I knew better, I said yes.

As you might imagine, the entire office team was new and hastily put together. This was the height of the dot-com boom. Almost anyone with confidence who knew how to get angel investors behind them could start a new business. It seemed as if everyone was scrambling to do so. Business models were nonexistent in many cases. These new executives thought that the sheer volume of Internet traffic would eventually bring in income but they had no foundation in place for the revenue. What they did well was sell others on their ideas. People scrambled to get hired at these high-tech companies, with the promise and vision of stock options as their golden parachute.

Be Alert to the Handwriting on the Wall

The new company hired its full staff within a few weeks. Everyone was unsettled because of the hastiness involved in building a company without policies and procedures in place. In some cases, computers and furniture had to be shared because those in charge did not have a handle on the rapid expansion. Selling an unknown brand of copier door-to-door sounded like heaven compared to this nightmare of a job. Predictably, the company soon experienced the revolving door syndrome, in which employees became so unhappy with management that they quit soon after they were hired. (It's interesting to note that this alone can cause a company to fold; indeed, the expenses of hiring, training, and rehiring are enormous.) So one by one, and sometime five by five, the employees quit. Some filed grievances due to unfulfilled promises. I was told there would be training, but the person in charge of training knew nothing about sales so it wasn't the least bit helpful.

At the end of my first week there, I was asked how soon my first sale would be coming in because they needed the money. Now, that was alarming! By the second week, Bill expressed unhappiness with my performance. To my astonishment I heard him say, "We discussed where your numbers should be by now and you have fallen far short. You will be fired if you do not improve your act." That was it for me. When shoved to the wall, I take action. The only smart thing I did was to keep the semi-used napkin featuring Bill's explanation of the compensation plan. That evening, I pulled out the wrinkled napkin and prepared myself to have a chat the next day with the human resources manager—a new low in my career.

Upon recognizing I wasn't just a misfit and that the company plan had indeed been misrepresented, The H.R. manager called Bill into her office. His face became flushed with embarrassment and astonishment when I proudly held up the napkin. To be fair, the H.R. manager put both of us on probation. The irony was that, within a month, both Bill and I quit on the same day.

At this point you might be thinking, *Well, that's sales. They all lie. That is not true for my industry.* I must acknowledge that salespeople generally are not held in high esteem, yet not everyone lies. And you may be in an industry in which only a small percentage of people misrepresent the truth. The purpose of my story about Bill is to advise you to proceed with caution, to pay attention to inconsistencies and oddities, and, most of all, to listen to your intuition. My intention is not only to get you a job, but to save you from potential grief down the road. This is just one example of how things can go awry.

A Fair Exchange When Selling Is a Must

A woman I'll call Jenny also had some challenges in an otherwise promising career. Jenny studied hard at a prestigious university. She was interviewed prior to graduation by a well-known accounting firm to consult with their top-tier clients. Learning that Jenny wanted to earn her MBA at another highly regarded institution, the company generously offered to pay her graduate school tuition. However, the generous offer came with a few strings attached, including a commitment to working for them for an additional three years after completing her degree.

Jenny accepted the offer, earned her MBA, and threw herself full swing into her job. Although it seemed glamorous at first to be flying from coast to coast on corporate jets consulting with household-name clients, it consumed much of her time. Jenny's personal life began to suffer. She tried her best to reconcile her work life and her personal life because she was under a several-year commitment to the firm. Eventually she got better at balancing the two. Jenny married a great guy and took a long honeymoon. Later that year, they needed to borrow additional time for a private family emergency. The agreement was that whatever time she took would be doubly owed to the firm.

A year later, recognizing the difficulty of the job and wanting a change of environment along with international travel, Jenny and her husband decided it might be fun to combine the two. She arranged to transfer to the company's Australian office. Life on the beach sounded great! The company moved the couple, all expenses paid, with the understanding that Jenny would give them an additional two years in return on top of what she already owed the firm. Life at the beach did not quite work out the way she envisioned it. In fact, the workload and the company politics were worse in Australia than they were in the United States. To top it all off, Jenny really disliked her new boss. She longed to return to her old job. While in Australia, Jenny needed to take maternity leave to tend to her newborn. The company agreed to support her in the transition but demanded she add another 12 months to her work commitment. The end of the story to date is Jenny is now heavily committed to a job and a company that she absolutely dislikes. It has had an adverse affect on her personal relationships. She is, in fact, completely overwhelmed by not knowing how to proceed from here. The moral of the story? Before you accept *any* offer, review all of the facts.

Jenny's story is a reminder to always keep in mind your own sense of fair play and know what you will and will not tolerate. Indebtedness should not be a requirement for employment. Once you realize you're unhappy and it is obvious you are not in sync with the company culture or politics, you would be wise to move on to try once again to find the more ideal spot.

At one point in my career, tired of selling business equipment, I decided to explore the possibilities of working in telecommunications, as that was the newest hot industry of the time. A friend I knew introduced me to a hiring manager she had worked with once upon a time. It was refreshing to hear my friend say she thought very highly of him. I viewed this particular interview as informational because I wasn't quite convinced I would be interested. If I were to change companies, I would need time to notify my current clients and transition out of my position. The hiring manager, whom I'll call James, was a very nice man. But some of his behavior gave me pause. To begin with, James avoided many of my questions. This did not sit well with me, as I believe in direct communication. And by the end of the conversation, he was pressuring me to accept his offer. My intuition said no, but my friend was taking a job at the same company. Once again, against my better judgment, I allowed her to talk me into doing the same. We would motivate one another to do well.

A few months later I learned that James had retired from his previous job that had provided him with an attractive pension. In his contract it was stipulated that if James were to work an additional 12 months for a partner company, he would collect an additional retirement bonus. This was his only motivation for occasionally showing up at the telecom office. His attitude toward his work and his team affected everyone negatively. He was rarely at work and was never available to answer questions. He simply did not care. If a team member needed help, he avoided being around until the request disappeared. It was a very aggravating job at best and, ultimately, it lasted only a short time until I called another friend in the business equipment industry and went to work for him. Again, the message here is to review all the facts and look before you leap.

Review Your Goals and Achievements

Interviewing for a job is an emotional roller coaster ride. It is for the strong of mind and the young at heart. If you are reasonably content where you are, then by all means stay. But if you are not being respected, if your voice is not being heard, if everything you attempt is shot down, if promotions are dangled like carrots but never materialize, and if promises are never kept—well, it's time to look for something better. If you give up and just settle, you will never know what was just around the corner

High tech proved to be even more unsavory than selling copiers door-to-door. The two high-tech companies that hired me both proved to be downright unethical. At the second high-tech company, I finally secured a position in which the base salary was meaningful and the job was cutting-edge, and I had a to-die-for clientele list waiting to purchase services from me. Only it turned out to be a new Seinfeld episode—a job about nothing. From the first day of employment I recognized empty promises had been made. By the end of the first week, I felt that my experience in high tech would be no different than it was in other industries. Only

I was wrong—my high-tech experience was much worse because it went against all of my rules for employment, including having solid ethics. Once I realized this, I immediately quit. However, I made one smart move before I walked out the door after resigning. (A salesperson has nothing if he or she foregoes his or her standard of ethics.) I headed straight for my cubicle and called every single prospect lined up to buy from me. Upon connecting with each, I first announced that I had just quit that very exciting project. I then advised them that after we hung up the phone, they should take five minutes to contemplate why I might have done that. Each prospect profusely thanked me for my call. This was about a month ahead of the dot-com bust.

As you interview, try to determine if the job will lead to a long-term career. As you can see from my own personal experience, it is disheartening to have to continually look for a new job. This is why it is so important to have your long-range career goals in mind when you interview. Ask yourself these questions:

- ℔ Will this opportunity advance my career?
- ℔ Does the position sound too good to be true?
- ℔ Does the job meet my qualifications for acceptance?

These examples are not meant to scare you but to bring a reality check into your interviewing process. Before each interview, determine if it will be a practice interview or if you really and truly want the job. Determine if the position is in alignment with your vision and your prioritized wish list. Will any of your principles be violated, or will you be able to advance your career goals upon acceptance of an offer? Will you be motivated to spend the day at work happily anticipating what each day will bring? You are the only one who can answer these very important questions. Be truthful with your answers and act accordingly. You will be glad you did.

Your thoughts sell you.

If you have been thinking *The competition is fierce*, or *There's a small chance I'll get this job*, or *I don't quite have the qualifications*, remember: Your thoughts sell you.

If any of these thoughts are running through your head, it will translate to your body language, facial expression, and speech when you interview. Any hesitation or awkwardness while answering will send negative signals to the interviewer, and any negative communication may ultimately dissuade the other person from hiring you. Charge your energy with "positive electrodes." Remember back to the childhood book *The Little Engine that Could*. The little engine's mantra was at first, "I think I can," and then changed to, "I know I can," and finished with, "I *knew* I could." Become that little engine that could. Many entrepreneurs will tell you that the secret behind *The Secret* is the power of positive thinking. Those who study metaphysics say we are part of a giant magnetic field, and whatever we put into our energy, we will receive in return. Whether you believe this or not, tell yourself *I am going to get that job* repeatedly before you go to sleep the night before your interview. Then sleep on it. You will wake up thinking, *I am going to get that job!* The subconscious mind is far more powerful than most of us give it credit for.

Once you've done all these things, you will be mentally prepared for the invitation to interview.

Be the little engine that could.

Selling Yourself Interviewing Tips:

- ✎ Reflect on the past to develop a better future.
- ✎ Remain true to your list of priorities.
- ✎ Check the facts before you accept.
- ✎ Do your best to remain analytical.
- ✎ Be on the alert for verbal and behavioral inconsistencies.
- ✎ Make certain all of your questions are answered.
- ✎ Read between the lines and listen for what is not being said.

- 🖐 Always listen to your intuition.
- 🖐 Always get everything in writing.

Goal-Setting and Planning

*T*he thought of selling anything sends shivers up the spines of most people. Selling yourself on an interview is even more frightening and represents more risk than most people are willing to consider, let alone engage in. However, when you approach sales as helping someone else solve their problems in a friendly manner, your fear will subside and you will be far more successful. Remain positive and focused, and remind yourself of the value you bring to the hiring company.

Overcome the Fear of Selling

First, **analyze your motivation to purchase and that of the person interviewing you**. Let me ask you something: Does making a purchase frighten you? Most people are quite good at making purchases! Take a moment to recognize that selling is a part of the same transaction as making a purchase; one person sells, the other purchases. So you have been around sales all your life! Take some time to think about each one of your past major purchases, and consider why you purchased from the person who made the sale. Did you feel coerced into purchasing? Did you like the personality of the salesperson? Why or why not? Was the purchase made to satisfy a need, or did it represent something on your wish list? Were you looking for value or a good deal and this person just happened to have it? It is safe to say all sales fill a need, satisfy a deep-seated desire, and/or present a good value. Are you comfortable purchasing new clothes, a car, or a home? Which part of the purchase-sales process convinced you that what you bought is a good value, was needed, or fits your desire? When you begin to analyze your past personal transactions, you will quickly see what motivates people to purchase. Likewise, when you are on a job interview, you will need to examine what motivates the interviewer to purchase. Once you make that determination, you will need to communicate how you will satisfy his or her needs and wants, as well as how you will bring outstanding value to the company.

Second, **determine your value**. When you start to doubt yourself, remember that you were likely chosen out of hundreds of applicants for the job. Your unique and special talents landed you that interview. Why? What is it that makes you unique and marketable? And, given all of your skills and talent, what is the salary range you deserve? Make a list of your top attributes, showing the value each attribute will provide to the hiring company. In each entry, make sure you address the issue of why the company should care about that attribute. The best way to communicate this is to review your past experiences and how your attributes affected the outcomes. Did you bring in additional clients, help move a failing project forward, or save the company money? Have very short examples ready to share that will illustrate these points and exemplify your value.

Another thing you can do to determine your value is to make a list of your career must-haves. When I meet with a prospect, I carefully consider whether he/she will be an ideal client. I believe life is too short to work with people you don't feel connected to in some way. When it comes to accepting a job, an additional important factor to consider is whether the project for which you are being hired sounds interesting and whether you will look forward to going to work each day, rather than dreading it. This list is what will make or break the sale from *your* point of view. Just as you might not purchase a car if it is not energy efficient, you will not take the job unless it offers x. Do not take this list lightly. The last thing you want is to have to go through the interviewing process all over again after you are hired.

Know who you are and what you want.

With this list in mind, you can then make a list of the factors that you would be willing to negotiate on prior to your accepting an offer. Rarely is any sale 100 percent to your advantage, so you have to determine what your deal-breakers are and where you are willing to bend. Using the car example, the mileage and size of the car might be right, but the color you want isn't available. Is that a dealbreaker, or will you move forward with the purchase anyway? Likewise, you most likely have a wish list for all of the bells and whistles you would like included in the job, such as a company cafeteria with free beer on Fridays. But if that isn't included, will you walk or accept anyway?

Third, it is also your job to determine what the company sees as its must-haves (non-negotiables) and to deduce its wish list in terms of you, the candidate. In sales-speak this technique is called **truthful matching**. Ultimately, you want to match your list (which you have naturally compiled with absolute truthfulness) with that of the company. Review your list before you go to sleep and when you first wake up in the morning. You must remind yourself during these quiet times why you are special and why you are the perfect person for the job. Then, affirm to yourself you will get the job because you know you can do it better than anyone else and bring new ideas to enhance what is required.

Fourth, **you must have a plan in place to achieve your goals**. Getting what you want in life first begins with a desire and then a plan to acquire or achieve that special something. Professional salespeople typically set fairly difficult goals for themselves and then establish a plan for achieving them. In your job search, always know where you are in the process and what remains to be done in order for you to get there. Just before you achieve your goal, establish new goals and plans so you can achieve even greater success. You simply cannot succeed if you do not have a laser-focused plan in mind. You must know what you want so that you can methodically go after it. Setting goals is the first step. Take a look at what the hiring company wants, to see if there is a match, and then find out how to communicate that match in the interview. Keep your list handy and update it as new ideas arise. Your list may look something like this:

My Interviewing Checklist

- ♮ My strengths
- ♮ My interests
- ♮ How others describe me
- ♮ Career aspirations
- ♮ Must-haves for the job
- ♮ Minimum and desired salary
- ♮ Acceptable company culture
- ♮ Items willing to negotiate

When you are compiling your list, take into consideration what you have loved to do since childhood. What have people always said about you? Are you unusual, interesting, or fun? Don't be shy about putting down all of your top attributes, even if they don't seem to be related to your upcoming interview. This list will help you to regain that initial excitement you felt when you heard you were chosen for the interview. Keep focusing on all of those positive attributes while you plan for a highly successful interview.

The list will also help you to further increase your confidence. Now that you have organized and formalized what is most important to you, you have some clear direction as to what will bring you the most job satisfaction in the next step of your career. As you read this book, keep your list of beneficial attributes, must-haves, and negotiable items handy. It will become a working document and the foundation for how you sell yourself. As you begin to interview, refine your list as new ideas and thoughts occur to you. The idea behind the list is to make sure you don't sell yourself short because you feel desperate for a paycheck. When you accept a position with major shortcomings, you will be in a worse position than you were in before you began.

Fifth, **take control of your career**. Many people make the mistake of saying to themselves, *This is what I'm stuck with; it's my unfortunate destiny*. This is very far from the truth. Others will treat you exactly as you portray yourself. When you take the lead and position yourself as an expert and a team player, others will begin treating you as such. Again, keep that positive mindset that you can and will succeed. Whenever you get down or others tell you that you are being too choosey, re-read the quote by Mark Twain and keep going!

Sixth, **turn rejection into opportunity**. One of the most important tenets of selling is to not take anything personally. In particular, do not take objections or rejection personally. It's a bit easier for salespeople to let rejection roll off their backs, because they can tell themselves it is what they are selling that was rejected, not them. It was business, not personal. When it comes to interviewing, however, your ego is at stake. It hurts when you are rejected, and it can feel very, very personal. If you are rejected and don't get the job, my suggestion is to step back and look at the whole experience analytically. Is there something you can learn from the process and improve upon the next time you interview? Ask yourself the following questions:

- Was I at all argumentative?

- Was my tone unpleasant when I was confronted with a particular question I did not appreciate?

- Did I hesitate when I was asked why there is a gap on my resume? Do I need to have a ready answer the next time I am asked this?

- Did there appear to be a personality conflict between me and the interviewer?

- Was I unable to overcome an objection, such as "You don't seem to have experience in..."?

Once your disappointment fades, it's important to realize that there is another opportunity waiting for you when you are ready to begin the process again. But before you begin, replay the entire interview leading up to the rejection.

Carefully analyze where the conversation may have hit a snag and, most importantly, how you might improve during your next interview. The following sales formula works whether you are a large company or an individual seeking work. When rejection occurs, use this three-step process for improved results the next time around:

- ✎ Analyze
- ✎ Tweak
- ✎ Get improved results

The final question to ask yourself is whether the job is truly a good fit for your experience and career goals. Chances are it may not have been a precise fit. It could be that something was missing. I believe that with every letdown or rejection, there is a better opportunity around the corner. As long as you can make it a learning experience, you can actually benefit from it and move on more confidently. In fact, many clients of mine have shared that due to their analysis for improvement, they were able to get an even better offer at the next company.

Seventh, **develop your own advisory board**. If you have trusted friends who are also unemployed and seeking work, ask them if they would like to form an informal advisory board to discuss their interviewing and job-hunting experiences with you. This could become a wonderful support group for all concerned, both professionally and personally. When your group meets, discuss elements of the past interview that you believe were troubling and ask for advice on how to improve. Of course, use your best judgment for which advice to follow! It can be a wonderful learning opportunity. The key element is to keep working toward improvement.

Eighth, **change your vocabulary from "failure" to "market research."** Most people unfortunately view their inability to get what they want as a failure. Instead they should copy the big corporations that, rather than stating that their latest model, initiative, or idea was a failure, will project a tone of authority by letting the public know that they did their market research and came up with something that will work even better. They never admit to poor planning in the first place; instead they focus on the new and improved solution. We should learn to do the same. Imagine how much more quickly you, too, will be able to move forward when you change your mindset and your vocabulary!

Ninth, **interview in the now**. Think of your previous rejection as the "before," turn your attention to the "now," and use your market research analysis for a better "after" result. Review your checklist. Your opportunity right in this moment is to more clearly define what will advance your career. Be honest if you need to refine your job search or just keep pursuing until you find that needle in the haystack. Anything worthwhile takes perseverance and the mindset that you can and will succeed. Not giving up and knowing that a new opportunity is waiting for you is the name of the game!

And finally, **selling yourself requires commitment**. Once again, you are prospecting to find that nugget of gold. Map out your goals for how many hours you plan to spend on job-hunting, calling past associates, networking, and follow-up. You must contact *everyone* you've met. How many days a week will you follow this plan? Commit to your answers and commit to your processes—you will have a much easier time.

Selling Yourself Interviewing Tips:

- ✎ Review why you were chosen for the interview.

- ✎ Determine your value.

- ✎ Use truthful matching to see if your goals and desires are in alignment with those of the company.

- ✎ Have a plan in place to achieve your career goals.

- ✎ Take control of your career.

- ✎ Turn rejection into opportunity.

- ✎ Develop your own advisory board.

- ✎ Change your vocabulary from "failure" to "market research."

- ✎ Interview in the now, with a mindset for success!

- ✎ Be willing to commit to the process of selling yourself.

Expanding Your Sales Funnel

*T*his chapter is meant to provide added insight and encourage creative thought on how you might find a job through non-traditional methods. I believe that as long as you remain polite and ethical, you are entitled to seek work wherever you want. To find the right job, you need to consider every possible company and position you can think of that might be a fit. Using stream-of-consciousness thinking works well in this regard. In a quiet place where you feel relaxed and willing to let your mind wander, think of career titles, endeavors, and hobbies that are related to your past or current work. Let your deep-seated dreams soar into the stratosphere and write those down, too. If necessary, devise your own "personal detours" for reaching your goals. For example, let's take a look at Janice.

Janice is a very capable administrator, yet she has been unable to get a job in her field. She finally decided to try selling cars. Many who knew her laughed because she just seemed too sweet and caring to be able to survive in auto sales. This was only partly true. Customers actually loved Janice because she is so sweet and caring. However, management did not, and kept changing the schedule on her so she never knew when she would be home to spend time with her teenagers. The next-to-last final straw came with her last test drive. She accompanied a prospective client who almost crashed the car with her in it. But the final blow came when money owed to Janice was withheld from her paycheck without a proper explanation. Once Janice realized that no one was willing to tell her when the money owed her would be released, she promptly quit. Still not able to get the job she wanted, Janice decided to turn her hobby of creating beautiful gift baskets into a business. It allowed her to be at home with her family, bring in a livable income, and do what she loves. Janice experienced a three-step detour but is now happier than ever.

While Janice was experiencing her topsy-turvy career detour, she was forever grateful to the people in her networking group. Her friends in the group provided advice for interviewing as well as how to handle the men at the dealership so they wouldn't take advantage of her sweet nature. They also encouraged her to give some thought to turning her hobby into a business.

As your list of target positions (your "sales funnel") grows, you will be much better equipped to find the best position. You may even find a unique niche that no one else thought of, thereby eliminating much of your competition.

If You Are Currently Employed

Have you ever wondered how to make the leap from employee to manager? To be management, you need to act like management. A client I'll call Bob exemplified the idea of transforming where you are today into where you wish to be in the future. Years ago, Bob was told that in order to be considered for management, it was necessary for him to dress and behave like a manager first. Bob mapped out everything he could think of that the management team did differently from the employees who reported to them, including himself. Once Bob had his list complete, he began implementing what he observed. Soon Bob began dressing and behaving like a manager. He was, in effect, bridging the gap between employee and manager because he was being *perceived* as a manager. In fact, upper management told Bob he was a better manager as an employee than most of the actual managers! Bob's behavior invited a formal promotion to management. The year-long planning and implementation of his action plan helped him achieve the first of his many career advancements.

Build a strong relationship with your manager

Another secret to getting ahead is to build a strong relationship with your current manager. Once you have proven yourself, have a heart-to-heart conversation as to what it will take to move up to the next level. Together, work out a plan of achievement to help you get there. Hold yourself and your manager accountable for your progress. Establish meetings at specified times. Check in with each other to ensure you're reaching set milestones. Regularly set new goals to help you get where you need to be for a promotion.

Make the process of selling a win-win.

The term "win-win" is used in sales when everyone involved feels as though they have won. Each person has received his or her desired outcome. Likewise, you always need to give some thought to the potential outcome of your actions. Keeping the win-win in mind, what would happen if the two of you worked closely together and your manager were promoted first? Because your manager has been basically grooming you for his/her position, you will be perfectly positioned to take over his/her slot as manager. To achieve this kind of long-term vision, your manager should become almost an accountability partner, if not a confidante. Work together to plan out what the two of you need to do to get to the next level. Upper management will be relieved to know that when they promote your manager they will not have to spend much time or money seeking someone to replace him/her. Instead, you most likely will be the automatic choice.

Change your position within the company

It is not always easy to switch positions within a company; indeed, it may take the same amount of effort as it would to interview at an entirely new one. However, sometimes it is in your best interests to stay where you are. For example, perhaps the childcare is excellent, or you are on track for retirement benefits, or maybe it's close to home and you don't want a longer commute. Given your motivation for switching jobs within the company, you first need to find out what the company policy is. In some companies, switching is not allowed, or, at best, it is frowned upon. You wouldn't want to begin a new job on bad footing.

Once you realize switching positions within a company is acceptable, let your current manager know in a private conversation this is your intention before you do anything else. Getting your current manager's approval will make the transition much easier. If you have a poor relationship with your manager, paint a positive picture that this proposal will be a win-win for the two of you. This should encourage your manager to help you in your quest. To be successful in your transition, you must build a relationship with your current manager (turn it around as best you can if it's not good) while building your relationship with the new intended manager. If you do not have a good relationship with your manager, consider applying for promotion in a different department. Is it time you became a manager and there just so happens to be an opening on another team? If you have a friend on the team with the open position, get the inside scoop from him or her. Find out if you will be a fit. If you believe you are a good fit, follow company protocol first. It could be that your current boss must approve the transition. If your relationship with your current boss is truly awful, it's possible that he/she might not want to let you go elsewhere. Instead, he/she may try to force you out. However, working to paint a picture of better times for both of you will go a long way to getting him/her to relent and work to help you switch.

Finally, approach the manager of the other team and ask what type of candidate they are looking for. If their needs sound like they would be a good fit for your qualifications, let the manager know you would like to apply. Generally speaking, as an inside candidate you have a better chance at getting the job than someone on the outside. By way of example, a friend and I both applied for jobs advertised at a local university on different occasions. Our interviews went really well and we both expected an offer. However, upon following up, we were told that someone from the inside had asked to transfer to the department at the last minute and that there was no longer a need for them to bring someone in from the outside. As a university they were required by law to post the position, so it would have been difficult for us to prove that the inside candidate had already been chosen prior to our interviews. However, we fully believe to this day that there was never any intention of hiring anyone from the outside. The point is that many companies prefer to fill positions from within. Consider this route as a stepping-stone for your career.

Complementary work helps advance your career

Another tactic for furthering your career is to step out of your chosen field and look for work in a complementary field. What this will do is give you a broader outlook on the field in general. You may even decide to continue on this new career path, or, once you have the experience you desired, you might go back to your original career and perhaps move up a couple of levels.

I took this route almost by accident and it worked out quite well for me. My original sales job was selling copiers and other business equipment door-to-door. It wasn't my ideal job but I needed to get started in sales and this was the one arena in which I could get hired after having stayed at home to raise children for so many years. When I accepted another job, this time for selling print services, it was complementary to selling copiers and printers. This work gave me an appreciation for how different departments in medium to large corporations use their equipment. I quickly learned the challenges they faced in turning out their work in a timely manner. It was fabulous inside information that could be leveraged when I eventually went back to selling networked printers and copiers.

Advance your career quickly by taking a calculated risk

Taking a calculated risk harms no one and can actually advance your career pretty quickly. When I interviewed at yet another company, the required experience was at least two years beyond what I possessed. I decided to apply anyway just to see what would happen. I wanted to know more about the company in question and what the title of "major account manager" entailed versus just being a sales rep. The manager of the department, whom I'll call Carl, appeared to be a nice guy, and we had a friendly chat per my interviewing style. While maintaining a professional demeanor, I treated him as if he were my new best friend. To my great surprise, I was offered the job. It ended up being the best job of my career. Carl admitted he knew the job was way past my capability at the time, but he liked my friendly style and thought my potential clients would, too. So he took a leap of faith and hired me.

Establish your expertise through vertical marketing

In "vertical marketing," you become an expert in one type of industry by learning its jargon, challenges, market trends, and any other pertinent information that comes your way. Informational interviews actually transform you into a vertical market expert and, ultimately, will help sell you in your "real" interviews. If you are pursuing a job in a new industry or if you've decided to jump a level or two in your field, you would do well to ask for informational interviews at competitive companies. Although you might be thinking that informational interviews take up too much of your valuable time, there are some benefits to consider. First, after a couple of practice interviews, you will have a very good grasp of how to interview well at your target company and what some of the challenges facing the industry might be. Second, the practice interview might go so well that you earn yourself a job offer! You could then have the advantage of two offers and the ability to negotiate a better package. So you have everything to gain by practice interviewing with industry competitors.

Find a sponsor or coach within your company

Salespeople are often advised to find a coach in large organizations. A coach will help guide the salesperson through the maze of the organization and provide helpful inside information. This relationship helps to increase sales. Likewise, within your current company, find a sponsor or champion who will benefit from helping you achieve your desired placement within the company. Remember, always work for the win-win so that others will be more inclined to help you. You may be able to connect with someone higher up in the organization through an extracurricular activity such as fundraising. Another option is to begin contributing to the company newsletter; in time you will be seen as the expert or go-to person in your department. There may be a call out to employees to help out with an important new campaign, and you might agree to volunteer or lead the brigade. Move full steam ahead on whatever commitment you make.

As the higher-ups see you take an active or leadership role, they might become your champions and groom you for the next level up the corporate ladder. You might become part of their inner circle and this can bring about rewards of its own. A wise team player will know to always thank his/ her coach for help and keep the coach in the loop while advancing through the hurdles. Your continued gratitude will keep the help coming your way. (Catering to someone's ego doesn't hurt, either!)

Attach your cart to the right horse

A number of years ago, an employee, whom I'll call Keith, predicted that his manager, whom I'll call Scott, would become the next vice president. Keith did everything possible to cater to Scott. His dream was that he would be promoted to take over Scott's management position when Scott moved into the VP role. Unfortunately, within six months it became apparent that Scott lacked many of the skills required to be a good vice president. He soon began to experience the slippery slope downward. Keith was caught in the middle of this turmoil. Because he never left Scott's side, he was viewed in upper management's eyes as being equally incompetent. Within those same six months, Keith had to seek other work outside of the company. The moral of the story is to know whom you are aligning yourself with!

If You Are Currently Unemployed

Conferences, trade shows, and events

You should be attending conferences, trade shows, and events. Most likely these types of events are occurring on a semi-regular basis in your area. These are fantastic opportunities for networking and doing some investigative work to find the right opportunity for employment. Some of the events will cost a considerable sum of money, whereas others will be open to the public. Your bottom line is important, so I would recommend beginning with the events that are either free or offered at very low cost, as long as they seem like they would produce good contacts for you. The events I am referring to are not necessarily job fairs. For example, you might attend a high-tech road show demonstrating the latest technology for sale, or you might find a health and beauty event featuring vendors associated with the industry.

When you attend these events, you will immediately spot the vendors at their tables or booths. Glance at their backdrops to read their offerings. Get a sense of whether a company interests you or not. Before speaking to anyone, read some of the literature on the table. Observe the people in the booth as you ask them questions. Try your best to understand what their business is about and if it might be a place where you would like to work. Do they appear to be friendly and helpful?

After a brief conversation, you will be able to determine if this company is of interest. If so, let the person in charge know where your interest lies. Ask them who would be the best person to speak with regarding an informational interview. Take the vendor's business card and write down the name and phone number of the person he or she suggests. Be certain to e-mail a thank-you to the person who helped you. When you contact the recommended party, tell him/her the name of the referring party, where you met, and why you are calling. If the referred party sounds friendly, ask when would be a good time for the two of you to talk or meet. If you can't meet in person, make the best use of your time on the phone. Ask if there is anyone else they think you should speak with. Before you end your conversation, make certain you know what your next steps are. As you progress through their system, send an occasional update and note of thanks for their help.

Part-time work

Another route is to take a part-time job. There are several benefits in taking this type of position. First, you experience first-hand the day-to-day reality of the company without making a major commitment. You will learn who the company officers and major players are, and meet the other employees (in a small company) or those directly involved with your work (in a larger one). If an opportunity for full-time work should present itself, this information will be invaluable in helping you decide whether you will enjoy working there.

Second, your part-time job may eventually turn into a full-time position. When you accept a part-time job and view it as an opportunity to put your best foot forward and prove yourself, chances are hiring managers will be pleased you walked in the door. You make it easy for them to see you, try you, and like you. When the next full-time job becomes available in your area of expertise, you will likely be the first one to be interviewed.

Third, a different full-time position than the one you originally sought may open up in the company. If you keep an open mind and think creatively, you may realize a better opportunity awaits you than the one you had originally planned for. Previously we spoke of taking positions that are complementary to your previous experience; the same applies in this situation. Rather than fixating on one career path, you expand your options and your career possibilities.

And finally, working part-time allows you to keep your skills current while you seek work elsewhere. If you have a highly specialized talent or one that is so general that you compete with thousands of other applicants (thus making the process of securing a job more difficult), part-time work is a good alternative. When you finally secure an interview, the last thing you want to hear is, "Because you have been unemployed for so long, your skills are outdated." Part-time work in your field will eliminate this objection.

Freelance work

An alternative to part-time employment is to do free-lance work for companies you are interested in. Due to the recent economic downturn, the chances are good that they have trimmed their staff substantially and thus recognize they might need extra help. They just don't want to pay for full-time help or the benefits that come with it. Your offer to do freelance work may be seen as a gift from heaven!

You never know until you ask.

I have a difficult time understanding people who predict that something is impossible or that it won't work. How do they know? If they can predict the future, why aren't they more successful themselves? There is nothing stopping you from approaching the companies you admire most and asking them if they have a need for your services on a freelance basis. Once again, this is your opportunity to get your foot in the door and prove yourself. Let me hammer the point home: *make it easy for them to say yes* when you apply for the next full-time opening.

Social media

A no-cost or low-cost way to find a job is through social media. Currently, the more popular sites are LinkedIn, Twitter, and Facebook. By offering snippets of your expertise online, you might encourage others to correspond with you. Not only are companies getting online, but recruiters are there, too. Helping others by providing sound advice will create interest and, very likely, some phone calls. Statistics show that a very high percentage of recruiters scour LinkedIn for potential candidates.

Have you thought about attracting further attention to your cause? If you already write a blog, articles, or a newsletter (all relatively low-cost endeavors), tweak what you write. Be certain to provide value to readers. At the bottom you can add an FYI to let the reader know you hope they enjoyed the information you shared. Add something to the effect of, "And by the way, I am seeking a position in x industry, in case you know of a company who would like to benefit from my talent."

Volunteering

Many people debate the pros and cons of volunteering for an organization with the end goal in mind of obtaining a full-time job with benefits. Let's examine the thinking behind donating your time to an organization. It's difficult sitting home alone day after day. You're probably lonely for conversation, and it's a tough adjustment to not have someone there to turn to for talking things over, particularly when you are feeling a little down. Listen to what your self-talk is telling you. If the negative feelings come in louder and clearer each day, you should definitely consider volunteering, if only to be among your peers again. In this case you have nothing to lose. An even stronger reason to volunteer is that you do not want your skills to become dated. No one can predict when the economy will turn around or when you will land your next job. If you are an engineer, for example, your skills need to be continually practiced and updated; continued education is a requirement. In this case it may be wise to consider volunteering.

Some companies may take you in as a volunteer or on a trial basis. If you believe you are right for the company and can make a difference there, it might be worth a try to volunteer and get to know the people who work there. With insight and creativity, you will be able to carve out a niche for yourself and sell yourself to management. In the meantime, you will get to know the players of the company, their processes, and how to maneuver within. It will take some time, but you can do it.

Timing is everything. Being at the right place at the right time will help you get what you want, particularly in your search for a job. With some luck and impeccable timing, you will find an agreeable management that wants to hire you after observing and benefitting from your excellent work. Being seen at the right time is where your luck needs to kick in.

Some people may believe that you should be spending all of your time looking for a job and that volunteering is a waste of time. Parents can be over-worried about their adult child moving back home due to the loss of a job. A spouse may be very worried that not enough income is coming in. He/she may feel upset that his/her spouse wants to volunteer and, in fact, may not see any wisdom in the decision at all. All of these people may be unrelenting, telling you that you need to be seeking work 10 hours a day, seven days a week. A lot of people close to you will offer these words of wisdom: "Why waste your time? You could be missing out on opportunity!" or, "You are never appreciated when you give your time away for free." In some cases there's no denying that these statements are true. It relates to the same principle that when services or products are sold too inexpensively, they can be perceived as having little value. If you offer to work for free, how can you expect to get a six-figure salary? It's a tricky thing. Be certain others are not taking advantage of you.

Working for free is definitely a gamble if you are ultimately planning on negotiating a high-paying job. A big concern about volunteering is that it is easy to go deeper into debt. Taking your budget into account, put a time limit on how long you are willing to work as a volunteer. The decision is yours to make. Whichever direction you decide to take, pursue it 100 percent. Half-hearted job-seeking never works; believe your strategy will work if you are given a fair chance or until you are proven wrong. If the worst happens and you are proven wrong, recognize that if you did not try, you would never know. Make it a learning experience. Remember to think like a major corporation—this is your market research to find what will or will not work.

Community service

My favorite suggestion to everyone, no matter where they are in life, is to devote part of their time to community service. Adapt your talents for what is needed in your local or greater community. For businesses, community service helps to spread good word of mouth; for individuals, it develops a grateful following; and for job seekers, it introduces them not only to people who appreciate their services but also nonprofits and other organizations that may have a hand in the organization they are helping. It gives them an opportunity to get in through the back door. Let me provide two examples, drawn from my own experience, of what one person and a collaborative effort can do to make a difference.

My personal experience is in the form of speaking to groups of job seekers on how to sell themselves on interviews. I have received notes of thanks expressing how appreciative the people were when they were chosen for a sought-after job due to the sales skills I taught them. It's heartwarming to know you can help others. Using Facebook, I reconnected with a friend, Christine LeMay, who is a brilliant career coach. She had the idea for the two of us to establish a career and business resource fair in our town. We were both fairly new to the community and wanted to meet new people as well as make a difference. Christine and I invited Kristi Frlekin, a branding guru, to attend because we knew she would be great at helping us spread the word about the fair. Although we did not know her, our mayor, Pam Torliatt, graciously agreed to provide opening remarks, and Kim Kasselonis, CEO of Circle Bank, agreed to be our premiere sponsor and provide a motivational talk to encourage our audience.

Our program was dedicated to helping job seekers understand that they are their own brand, identifying and explaining the factors they should consider when deciding to accept a job, and explaining why and how they should sell themselves on interviews. Each of us included advice to inspire and motivate our attendees to keep moving forward. The *Argus Courier*, our local newspaper, provided excellent coverage beforehand, helping us to draw a crowd of about 200 people. More importantly, they became 200 grateful people who left motivated to succeed. Ultimately, the experience provided me with the motivation to write this book. So ask yourself: What can you do to translate your skills into helping others in your community, and where will that take you ultimately? In my opinion, it can only help you in your search for a job.

Networking

Networking well requires a decent command of marketing. As we discussed previously, how you look, how you act, what you know, what you say, and how you say it all contribute to creating your unique brand. Other people will make judgment calls about you based on these factors, and will quickly decide whether or not they want to help you.

Selling requires you to put your best foot forward.

In order to improve others' perception of you, it would be wise to take the extra time to practice your communication style in front of a mirror. Check that you have the following:

- ✤ Good posture
- ✤ A genuine smile
- ✤ Friendly body language
- ✤ Precision of language

Most people are so focused on their need for income that they forget to smile. Even their body language and gestures are less than friendly. This can leave a negative impression on people you meet, and prevent you from securing leads for a job that you want. Nonverbal communication cues are a part of your brand development. The same is true for every stage of the job-seeking and "selling-yourself" process. Improving your communication skills will work greatly to your advantage. By embracing the significance of these cues and acknowledging the effect they have on others, you can turn every meeting into a positive experience and increase your chances for getting hired.

Networking can either be frustrating or highly rewarding. It all depends upon your frame of mind and the attitude of those around you. When you find the right group it becomes highly rewarding. Many people ask why they should network with people who are out of work, and wonder if it will be depressing. Certainly, if you find that depressing, don't do it! However, what if you could find a group that's fun to be with? What if you hold common interests? What if the group has contacts for you to follow up with?

Wouldn't these possibilities make some of these events worth attending?

Research what groups are available in your area. The only note of caution is to visit a couple of times and weigh what you get out of attending versus the real cost of time and money. Ask for recommendations from associates and friends and visit a few different groups to find the best fit for you. The biggest qualifier of all is whether or not the group is receptive and interested in helping each other. Determine if you will find the support you need, both personally and professionally.

Groups exist for almost every type of business or industry you can think of. You don't have to stick to groups of people who are out of work. Consider joining a group for your preferred industry, a community service group where you can make a difference, or even a group that concentrates on your leisure interests. There is something out there for everyone. When you are unemployed, it can be very depressing to sit, day after day, in front of your computer looking at the job boards. You have to get out and make new friends and open up more channels for communication. The more connected you become, the greater the number of opportunities that will come your way.

Now that you are about to start attending networking events, have a plan for how you're going to tell people exactly what you are looking for. You *are* your marketing effort. Practice what you're going to say for effective communication.

It is important to capture attention with your opening statement, or *tagline*. Brevity and concision are of utmost importance here. However, you also want be able to portray

Marketing precedes sales!

your unique self and come across as genuine. Think of a 10-second introduction that will relate exactly what you do and attract interest. Once the words leave your mouth, you want to hear the other person ask, "Can you tell me more?"

My own experience attending networking events was an eye-opener. Upon proudly announcing I was a sales trainer, one of two things usually happened: the men were dismissive, believing there was no way a woman could know enough about selling to be a trainer; and the women could not run to the exit sign quickly enough because of the ugly connotations surrounding sales. After I began devouring marketing materials, however, I learned the essential marketing communications strategies to attract business. Instead, I would say, "I help my clients increase revenue by teaching relationship selling." Generally speaking, the phrase "increasing revenue" caught the attention of the men, and "relationship selling" attracted the attention of the women.

What can you say that will draw attention when you announce what you do? Practice with friends to help you transform your tagline into something catchy, and be sure to have a two-minute story to back it up when they request that you tell them more (which they will!).

You have a 10-second tagline and a two-minute story waiting to be told.

Think about the 100 people who might be vying for the same job you want. What makes you different from them? How do you approach work, organize projects, and meet deadlines? What has been your experience? Do you have any interesting stories to share? Remember, your stories should be kept to a one- to two-minute timeframe. No one wants to be bored to death by listening to you talk about yourself excessively!

Sell the unique you

Knowing how you differ from everyone else in your field means that you know your competition. If you are experienced in the workplace you should be aware of how you deliver your services differently than others doing the same job. If you just graduated and are new to the workforce, reflect on what made you stand out in class. How were you different from the other students? What motivated you to graduate? Which classes did you like best, and why? Do any of your hobbies relate to some of the classes you took?

Let me explain from my own perspective why these reflective questions are important. Personally I did not care for school, so I set my goal to secure a university degree in four years. No matter what, I would be out of there within that time frame. The only way I could make it through was to take anthropology and archaeology classes. I always loved to travel and still do. I enjoy meeting people of all cultures, and these classes catered to those interests. All of this translated extremely well to my sales career. It is my ability to find common interests with all types of people and to communicate effectively that has helped me achieve success.

When you remain true to your interests, your schooling and career will be in accord and bring about greater reward and satisfaction. So when you talk to an interviewer about what motivated you at school, do so in terms of why your classes were relevant to your current interest and skills and how they address the hiring company's needs.

Your past experience sells you.

All of your past experiences come together to help form your personal brand. They are what make you unique. When you can express your uniqueness well, it will attract others to you. It is your personal marketing message. Fellow networkers will provide you with leads and hiring managers will exclaim, "You offer exactly what we are looking for!"

Women: take note

Women have one extra step to take care of before they march into a networking event where men will also be in attendance. When a man asks you for your contact information to send you job leads, and you begin to fish in the bottom of your purse for a business card or pen, it looks very unprofessional. The man may become impatient and regret that he offered to help. Do yourself a huge favor and leave your purse in the trunk of your car. Additionally, you do not need a brush, comb, or makeup, or pictures of your grandchildren, or a wallet containing all of your identification. All you need is the clothes on your back and two pockets. These two pockets are sufficient to carry your business cards, a pen for note taking, and the cards of others who offer help.

You may also purchase a small leather-bound tablet that looks professional and contains pockets for your business cards and a holder for your pen. These are readily available, usually at a considerable discount, at office supply stores. The tailored binder will add to your businesslike image and show that you are ready to take action should a hiring manager happen to be in the room. It is important to remember that you never know whom you might meet.

Be hospitable

Many people believe that networking is a numbers game. They assume that the event is not successful unless they meet most of the people in the room. I disagree. When you approach the event with this mindset, most of your conversations will hold little value because you will be in too much of a hurry to move on and meet the next person. A better approach is to take the time to understand and get to know each person you interact with. Figure out how you can help each other or, at the very least, learn from each other. Being open to suggestions and direction from everyone around you is the quickest path to success. It's also the least expensive way to get the help you need! All in all, focus on quality versus quantity.

When you interview, the best way to begin a conversation is to ask the other person a question. Apply this to networking and you will have far greater success. A question that works every single time is, "What type of job are you looking for?" Rarely does any technique work all the time, but this particular question should jump-start the conversation because it goes to why everyone is at the function in the first place. Additionally, by asking the other person a question and letting him or her speak first, you will find out if he or she is competing with you for a similar job. You might also find out that you're in complementary fields and are able to suggest new ideas to each other. Or, you may also just find a new friend and mutual support system.

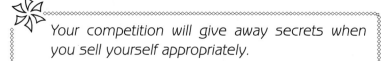

Your competition will give away secrets when you sell yourself appropriately.

I have a word of advice about meeting your competition face-to-face at these events. Although it may be difficult to spend your time talking to these folks at first, let them do most of the talking to learn about where they are interviewing, the sites they use for job searches, and other events they attend. Let them brag all they want. They may give you valuable information that you wouldn't otherwise have had. Clearly this tactic is to your benefit.

Use bragging to your advantage

On the opposite end of the spectrum, some people are very guarded about the information they share, and you will spot this immediately. Move on. Do not feel obliged to waste your time. Of course, always be polite and thank the person for his or her time, but move on quickly. Seek out the people who are willing to share *quid pro quo*. Smart salespeople always work for the win-win. The same goes for job seekers.

Everyone has a different perspective on networking events. Some people find a gathering of unemployed people depressing, whereas other people truly enjoy these events because they find value in learning from the speakers and the people around them. They find comfort in the fact they are not alone. Determine which category you belong to and proceed accordingly.

Alternatives to job-seeking groups

If you are in the first category and find it depressing to network with groups of unemployed people, it might be wise to find other groups that may be a better fit. For instance, if you are an architect, find associations where architects network. Very often, even if there is a fee involved, they will let you visit once or twice before requesting that you join their organization. Think creatively about where you might meet someone that can help you find a job or a group that might be helpful and motivational. In your personal life, do your best to spend time with positive people. This can improve your attitude and positively affect how you approach your job search during working hours. The Small Business Association (SBA) has free resources available, including classes on effective job-hunting, career counselors on staff, and guest speakers to give you the latest information from their field or how to find employment. This is one offering definitely worth investigating.

Selling Yourself Interviewing Tips:

- Create your own opportunity.
- Advance at your current company.
- Volunteer on projects in order to be seen.
- Adapt your skills for community service.
- Create a goal path with your current manager.
- Interview with different departments.
- Seek out venues where potential employers are gathered under one roof.
- Thank every person who helps you and provide them with status updates.
- Freelance!
- Seek part-time work for paying bills and keeping a positive mindset.
- Call everyone you know to ask for advice, suggestions, and help.
- Develop a 10-second tagline and two-minute story for networking events.
- Have your goals in mind before attending an event.
- Determine if the group is right for you.
- Weigh the expense of networking against the value.
- Let the other person speak first.
- Offer help to as many people as possible.

4

Developing Your Brand

ales and marketing and interviewing strategies overlap in a number of areas. The one area that is arguably most important to you as the job seeker is developing your unique brand, or, in sales terms, "positioning." Your brand is what distinguishes you from everyone else. As an individual, your words, actions, and deeds come together to create your brand, or unique selling proposition. All of these have to be in sync to demonstrate integrity and build credibility and trust. You must be as consistent as a box of cereal.

Dress for Success

When people contact you for any type of job, they should know upfront exactly what they will be getting. Some of this can be demonstrated in your choice of clothing and accessories. When you get dressed in your favorite outfit and step in front of a mirror to give yourself the once-over, does an automatic smile come to your face? Do you give yourself the nod of approval? What does that feeling do for you? Do you become more energetic and a little happier with yourself? Now imagine yourself as you enter the interview: Will you automatically attract others by your style, whatever it may be? Are you dressed appropriately for the occasion? Do you portray the aura of a highly qualified person with a distinctive personality? Your brand should position you above the competition just by virtue of the fact that you are you. To do so, you must really understand the true you to build your brand.

Years ago I owned a bright red suit. Most people were wearing either dark blue or black suits at the time. Whenever I knew the time was right to make a sale or land a job, I wore that suit. Each and every time, everyone commented how good it looked on me. From their input, I knew it attracted the right attention and it gave me an added air of confidence. My suggestion is to think about what you own—everything from your clothing and shoes to your briefcase and choice of jewelry—that will do the same for you. The clothing and accessories you wear represent your brand.

A note of caution regarding perfume and cologne: when you are getting ready for an interview, keep in mind that many people are allergic to colognes and perfumes. For this reason, it's best to skip it altogether. If allergies aren't reason enough for you to forego your favorite scent, keep in mind that everyone's tastes and olfactory senses differ. You may wear a fragrance that is distasteful to the interviewer. Some people are so sensitive that they will not want to be in the same room with you. In short, nothing is to be gained by wearing a scent. And of course there are food smells that some can find offensive, as well. My husband has had people come in for interviews after they've eaten both garlic fries and onions. Needless to say, their breath wasn't the best! Word to the wise: keep breath mints on you at all times.

Thoughtfulness

The moment you arrive at the location of your interview, everyone will be monitoring you. If there is a doorman, smile and say thank you as you come inside. When you spot the receptionist, approach him or her with a big smile and explain that you have a meeting scheduled. Thank the receptionist for his or her help. Should someone escort you to the meeting room, have a light-hearted conversation about how they like working at the company. You might gain some insight into the social atmosphere. As you approach the meeting room, thank the person for his or her insight and help in finding the room. In other words, the phrase "thank you" is one of your best marketing and selling tools. It lets others know you are polite and appreciative of their help, and they most certainly will let the decision-makers know their feelings about you. With your thoughtfulness you are also selling the fact that you are easy to work with and a team player. All of this serves to increase your interviewing score. Your final score is what will differentiate you from the rest of the competition. Of course, you still need to continue building your brand *during* the interview. If you are applying for a customer service position and claim you are excellent at building relationships with clients, you had better demonstrate those skills during the interview.

I am also a strong believer in avoiding any unforeseen incidents such as the dreaded ringing cell phone. To avoid this, leave your cell phone in your car. If you don't have a place to leave it, make sure it's turned off. Also, don't text or e-mail as you wait for your interview. Normally this would be a good use of your time, but in this case you are waiting for an interview and your future is at stake. It would be a far better idea to observe what and who is around you. Essentially, anything you can do to demonstrate that you possess etiquette and thoughtfulness (in addition to talent, skills, and a desire for the job, of course) will develop your brand and increase your likelihood of getting ahead of the competition.

Assume the Sale

Until your interview begins, the time is yours to demonstrate your interest in the company. Part of getting the job is assuming the role (sale). To do this, roll up your sleeves and dig in *before* the interview. In fact, I advise you to arrive 10 minutes early for your appointment to take in all you can. (But do not arrive any earlier or the company will think you have nothing better to do.) As you wait, you may note awards, client letters, interesting magazines, letters to shareholders, and of course the general demeanor and dress of the employees. All of these will help you gather the information you need to connect with your interviewer and assume the sale.

Tell a Story

In addition to confidence and preparedness, there are other secrets to connecting with your interviewer. A technique that I learned through a Dale Carnegie public speaking class is that storytelling attracts greater interest in you and what you are saying than just a mere recounting of facts does. As long as you keep the story short (one to two minutes maximum) and it is truly germane to the conversation at hand, you will see the relationship between yourself and those interviewing you begin to build. Have an interesting story ready to go if you are ever asked on an interview how you chose the field you are in. Tell the story with passion and emotion, and make it genuinely your own. Never memorize a script! People buy your "brand" and hire *you*; a scripted story will sound disingenuous. But if you relay your story with believability and feeling, you will become far more likeable in the eyes of the interviewer.

During an interview with a director of sales for a print services rep position, I was asked why I chose to go in to sales after being a stay-at-home mom for so many years. Caught unawares, I shared the story of how, after I realized I had to return to work, my husband announced to me one evening,

"I know what you should do. You have the personality of a salesperson!" I told the interviewer that I was horrified and had turned around to ask him, "Is that a compliment or an insult?" Ironically, I actually had a very negative opinion of salespeople at that time. Clearly, it was terrible thing to say during an interview for a sales job, and I was mortified. Luckily, the laughter in the room could be heard down the street. My story was told with innocence and genuineness, which made it relatable. Management felt that if I could make them laugh like that, the customers would love me. I soon heard the words, "You're hired!" However, the lesson here is to think ahead about what you are going to say. What is most interesting about why you chose your field? Your interests, passions, childhood experiences, places you have been—how did all of these factors contribute to the great story you will tell on your next interview?

Make Friends

Relationship-building and selling apply to every opinion you express and every request you make, whether in business or in your personal life. When I first began in sales, I heard the same phrase over and over again: "People buy from people they like." Take a moment to think about the last time you purchased an item from someone you didn't like. How did you feel? Did you go back to that salesperson ever again? I'm willing to bet the answer is no. Now take a moment to think about one of your favorite companies that you purchase from frequently. Why is that? Are the salespeople friendly? Do they provide a great service or product? Is their customer service policy excellent? Chances are the biggest reason is because you *like* them. For your interviews it's important to find a style you like best and make it your own, but the likeability factor has to be there. We all have our moments, particularly when we are stressed, so the best thing you can do is increase your awareness of how you come across to others during these stressful times, in order to portray the most relaxed and friendliest side of your personality.

The same principle applies to business communication. Most people believe you have to be businesslike at all times, but that is simply not true. Everyone loves to talk about themselves, their families, and especially their vacations. If you receive an e-mail from the person who will be interviewing you, stating that he/she will be away on vacation and must therefore delay your interview, your best move is to respond not with disappointment, but with best wishes for a wonderful vacation. And when you finally meet, ask how the vacation was and let him/her enjoy telling you. The friendliness will work to your advantage. If by chance you have visited the same locale, say so! This is a great way to make a connection and create a foundation of shared experiences. My only caution here is that if you are the least bit competitive, you will have to be very careful not to let drop that you went to fancier restaurants, took more expensive tours, or stayed at a nicer hotel. It is an easy trap to fall into; salespeople in particular can easily lose sales because of their competitive natures. You can never go wrong being respectful and aware of what the other person is telling you.

In short, you will become a more interesting person and a more appealing candidate in the interviewer's eyes when you communicate as a friend. Taking an interest in the interviewer's personal life will put you ahead of your competition, and there's a very good chance that the interviewer will see you as a fun addition to his or her team.

Communication Style

A big part of your brand involves how you communicate. Prior to your interview, hone your communication style. Practice with your friends and ask for feedback. Stand in front of a mirror to observe your facial expressions, body language, and gestures. Statistics show that *how* you say something actually has more impact than *what* you say. Again, friendliness adds to that impact and impression. You want to be memorable, and you want that memory to last. My own communication style is direct and candid. For example, when I was selling print services to large corporations, a number of appointments landed me in the Marcom departments of those companies. At one such company, I was introduced to a guy I'll call Jim. He was a very friendly fellow and I felt comfortable with him, so I felt no embarrassment when I asked him what his title, Marcom Director, meant. Most people would rather lose business than ask that kind of question, but I'm never afraid to admit that I do not know something, and this always works to my favor. Indeed, my forthrightness is part of what makes me unique. Jim actually appreciated the question. He proudly told me it meant marketing communications, and went on to describe his job and all that it entailed. My honesty built trust between us, so he gave me the inside scoop on the department. My question created a win-win: Jim felt great and I got what I needed to know. We had a fantastic conversation. By the end of our first appointment, Jim handed me a rather large print job. From that moment on we were friends, and his work flowed continually into my hands. Upon my return to the office, I asked that the title on my business cards be changed to Marcom Print Specialist. With the inside information Jim shared, I was easily able from that point onward to get appointments with the heads of Marcom in many of the Silicon Valley companies.

Solve their problems

Successful business is conducted in an almost formula-based sequence, and if you adapt your communication style to this formula it will serve to build your relationship even further during the interview. When companies experience challenges, they surmount them in the following sequence: problem • analysis • solution • results. When interviewers ask you tough questions, your answers should follow this basic outline. They will be impressed you are familiar with the magic formula. They will be convinced that you know how to look at any given situation, are able to analyze how it may be fixed for the better, and can easily implement the solution for greater results. Have several example situations in mind before you appear on your next interview. It will impress your interviewers and keep them engaged. You will be speaking their language and making them feel right at home with you, which is exactly where you want to be.

Honesty Is the Best Policy

If you make any kind of claim regarding your expertise on your resume, you must be able to back it up with fact if you are questioned about it. For example, Bill, a hiring manager, was well known at his company for the ability to put gibberish in his conversation when speaking with new candidates regarding open positions. This was his method of weeding out candidates who lacked integrity. One day, a job-seeking engineer was in Bill's office and nodding yes to everything Bill stated. The engineer even said he was very familiar with Bill's made-up terms. Obviously he did not get the job. When you are confronted with something that is unfamiliar to you, just ask the interviewer what he or she means. Don't worry about appearing ignorant; hiring managers will actually appreciate your willingness to be open to new ideas and admit when you do not know something. This will demonstrate to them that you are transparent and humble. Honesty is always the best policy.

Make Suggestions

Given the job description, are there suggestions you can make to enhance the position when the time is appropriate? Don't be shy about making suggestions. Suggestions can be offered in question form—for example, "Have you ever thought about x?" Whether or not the interviewer seriously considers your idea, it will at least demonstrate you have given the position some serious consideration of your own. This again works toward developing your brand as an innovative employee who is willing to take the time to learn, to analyze, and to develop new solutions. Your leadership capabilities will also become evident here.

Ask for Help

Asking for help is another way to build your brand. It makes those you are asking feel important, and by carefully listening to their advice, you demonstrate you are eager to learn and be a team player. This builds your relationship with them and boosts your integrity quotient. These are all virtues that will help you make the sale and get hired. If you are newer to the workforce, find others who are a few years ahead of you in experience who might be willing to help you. Do your best to seek out people in your field and ask what the expectations at their company are and what they need to do to exceed them. If you happen to know someone inside the company you are interviewing for, you will gain a big advantage by asking him/her questions such as:

- ♮ "Why do you believe you got this job?"
- ♮ "What do you think put you ahead of all the other candidates?"
- ♮ "Are there any additional words of wisdom you can share with me about interviewing and working here?"

When you ask these questions, the person may be even more inclined to help you get the job. As a thank-you for his/her assistance, offer to take him/her out to lunch. He/she will be forever grateful.

Understand the Mindset of the Hiring Company

Sometimes the hiring company will require you to take a personality test. Some of these are several pages long and often ask the same question from many different angles to check for consistency and honesty. Your answers will also reflect whether or not you are suited for the job. Herein lies the paradox: should you give the answers that you think they want to hear, or should you be 100-percent truthful even if you think it will cost you the offer? I asked a few of my fellow experts about the following situation I encountered, and all of them firmly disagreed with my choice. However, I was the one who heard "HIRED!" Read the story and decide for yourself what you would do under similar circumstances:

I was applying for a major account sales position that would require me to develop a new territory and call on Fortune 100 corporations. In my interview, I was asked, "Would you rather be an ice cream truck driver or a kamikaze pilot?" Now, the idea of risking my life as a kamikaze pilot is not my ideal situation! However, although driving an ice cream truck sounded like fun, selling is all about risk-taking and implementing untried tactics to get the sale. Therefore, I chose "kamikaze pilot" as my answer. When I was called in to sign the contract of employment, my manager-to-be said, "I don't know whether I should be thrilled to pieces you are now on my team or if I should be scared to death of you!" The end of the story is that it was the best job I ever had.

Plan to Exceed Expectations

The last piece to consider in developing your brand is your final result. The typical employee review is in the form of a report card, but instead of letters that you received in school, these reviews feature categories such as "unsatisfactory," "average," and "exceeds expectations." Whether you are new to the workforce or more experienced, it is a good idea to have this review in mind while interviewing for a job. Before you walk into any interview, strategize beforehand what you can do to show them that you fit into the "exceeds expectations" category. When you do this well, you cannot help but succeed.

Selling Yourself Interviewing Tips:

- Develop your brand.
- Dress for success.
- Be thoughtful, and use proper etiquette.
- Assume the sale.
- Connect by telling a story.
- Make friends with your interviewer.
- Hone your communication style.
- Solve the company's problems.
- Make suggestions.
- Be honest at all times.
- Ask for help.
- Understand the company's mindset.
- Plan to exceed expectations.

Prospecting

The sales term "prospecting" may bring to mind to an old-time prospector looking for gold. As a prospector in your job search, you search everywhere imaginable for the "gold" (prospects) and analyze every possible outcome. In this way, you come closer and closer to finding the ideal company to interview with.

Prospecting can be done in a variety of ways, such as calling someone on the phone, e-mailing, sending a letter, networking, asking for informational interviews, and even the old-fashioned method of knocking on doors unannounced to find out more about a company (in selling terms this is referred to as "cold calling"). Of all of these, my friend and colleague Rebecca Kieler, of Kieler Career Consulting, is adamant that your highest success rate will be found through networking. This means that you need to tell everyone you know and everyone you meet that you are looking for a job. Most importantly, you must be able to easily and clearly communicate exactly what you are seeking. A very easy way to start networking is to make a list of all of your past associates and current friends who have moved on to new companies. Then, call each and every person on the list! Then, you can start reaching out to potential contacts whom you don't already know.

The Friendship Approach

This is very similar to when a long-lost friend calls you unexpectedly. The first words out of your mouth most likely are, "What's new?" Rather than taking control of the conversation from the outset, you want to know what's going on in his or her life and why he or she has decided to call you after so many years. By posing your questions and putting the conversation ball in his or her court, you allow for a friendly catch-up and get some insight into the motive behind the call. Once you know why your friend called, you will be able to communicate more effectively. Similarly, as a salesperson, you need to get into the mindset of the other party so that you know how to position what you have to say. People buy in to what you have to say when they feel a connection with you. The commonality builds trust and confidence, two of the motivating factors behind making a sale.

> *Every prospecting step must begin from the other person's point of view.*

Before you even pick up the phone to speak to a potential contact, have a plan about what you're going to say. Even before you announce who you are, I find the best approach is to let that person know that you just visited his or her Website. Imagine that you work in marketing, but the P.R. and advertising personnel were laid off and you have to do their jobs plus your own job. How excited would you be to talk to a stranger who is disrupting your workday asking questions that you care very little about? "Not very" is the likely answer. So when you call a potential contact, a ringing phone that interrupts his or her workday, combined with hearing a stranger's voice (yours) at the other end, will very likely encourage that person to get off the phone as quickly as possible. By using the friendship approach, however, the other person may be more inclined to hear you out for a few seconds. Make your comments believable and provide a solid enough question for that person to want to continue the conversation!

Remember how I first had you enter into the feelings and thought processes of the other person? Every single step must begin from the other person's point of view. For example, if you start by saying that you like the focus of his/ her company and/or that you relate well to something on its Website (such as its mission or vision statement), you might find that he/she will stop and listen to you. You're calling for a reason, and you've obviously done some research—this lends to your credibility. Once you've steered the conversation to the company with your opening statement, tell your contact who you are, and be certain to explain how your statements about the Website relate to your job search. Next, tell your contact you were hoping to chat for just a few minutes or to set an appointment to have a future conversation on the phone or in person. Again, being considerate of the other person and his/her lack of free time will be appreciated. Chances are, he/she will speak with you or set a time to do so.

Avoid Telemarketing Techniques

I personally challenge you to think of two people who think exactly alike on all subjects. We are all unique human beings. Therefore a script will not work to your advantage because everyone takes in information differently. *Do not* read from a script. The all-time best sales technique is the anti-sales approach. You must sound natural and low-key, as if you were speaking to a good friend. Do your best to relax and smile—this will relax the other party and create a willingness to listen, if only momentarily.

> *The all-time best sales technique is the anti-sales approach.*

Following are a few examples of what a good prospecting call might sound like. Please remember to adapt any suggestions to your own vocabulary and style so it sounds authentic. In every call, listen for what is said and what is not said. The more astute you become as a listener, the greater success you will enjoy in all forms of communication.

✎ **Scenario #1: The voice answering the phone sounds exasperated.** You say, "I was on your Website and am impressed by your mission statement and customer service policies. My name is_____. I would love to talk with you for a few minutes but you sound rushed—is there a better time to call you, or would you have just a couple of minutes now?"

✎ **Scenario #2: The voice answering the phone sounds calm.** You say, "I just visited your Website and am impressed both with the new technology you offer and by your clientele. I work in the same field and am seeking a new position. My name is_____. Would you have a few minutes to talk now, or may we set an appointment to meet to discuss what you are seeking from your next employee?"

✎ **Scenario #3: You are speaking to the hiring manager about a specific job posting.** You say, "Your job posting spoke directly to my talents and interests. My name is_____, and at your convenience, I would love to come in for an interview. The job sounds like a perfect fit for both of us!"

Did you notice that I don't suggest mentioning your name until at least the second sentence ? If you were to announce your name first, you may be cut off with "We don't want any!" and find yourself getting hung up on. Instead, by delivering the suggested opening sentence first, you will catch the person's attention and interest. Most importantly, your question will help transition that person's attention away from what they were concentrating on and toward the conversation with you.

The last step is to create a bridge between their needs and what you have to offer, which hopefully will attract enough interest for you to be invited in for an interview. At the very least, you want to secure a phone interview if that is their first requirement. Never make a phone call just after you have received bad news or when you are feeling discouraged. I learned long ago that you must be 10 times more enthusiastic on the phone than you are in person. The enthusiasm comes over the wire and can often encourage people to be more willing to speak with you.

Demonstrate an Easy-to-Work-With Nature

Conflict in the workplace is commonplace and creates commotion and chaos. A critical issue for the company can be wasted time that is spent trying to resolve conflicts. The mediation process eats up time and money. A company's biggest fear is often a potential lawsuit by a disgruntled employee. Understanding this underlying theme of wanting good-natured employees is very important for your interviewing debut and subsequent meetings. How can you improve your easy-to-work-with image over the phone? Some pointers I learned along the way include the following:

✎ Begin with a huge smile—even though they can't see you! Keep a mirror nearby to make certain you continue to smile through the entire call. Smiling can soften your voice.

✎ Stand up while you speak. This can provide added energy. You'd be amazed at the difference in your tone standing up versus being curled up on a sofa.

✎ Take a brisk walk outside before you call. If it's raining or cold and you can't get outside, call a good friend or do jumping jacks to get your adrenaline pumping.

Each of these techniques will help you start the conversation in a friendly manner and come across as very upbeat. All of these suggestions encourage the person on the other end of the phone to speak with you.

Encourage Communication in All Forms

Voice mail is important, too. When you leave a voice mail, the same principles apply, and your voice should still reflect the same friendly tone. Voice mail does have its own additional set of rules, however:

✎ Be succinct and leave a very short message.

✎ Provide your phone number twice in case the volume fades in and out.

✎ Express the same interest in the company's Website and provide your name and the reason for your call.

Voice mail and e-mail used together yield a higher response rate.

There are some strategies you can use to get a higher rate of return than you would for just an e-mail or voice mail. Part of the secret is to use both. Here's how you do it: At the end of your succinct voice mail, let the other party know that you will send a follow-up duplicate e-mail. (Of course, only do this if you actually have his/her e-mail address and plan on following through on this promise.) Then, in the subject line of your e-mail, write: FOLLOW-UP TO PHONE MESSAGE. Although the other person does not know you, he/she will be anticipating your message.

Keeping promises = credibility = trust = sales (or, getting what you want!).

The first paragraph of your e-mail should indicate that you recognize that he/she is busy and that replying to the message may be easier and quicker than calling back. This alone sends an underlying message that you value his or her time. Tell him/her very briefly in the second paragraph exactly what caught your eye on the company's Website, why you are contacting him/her, and that you would like to arrange an appointment. Make it easy for the person to read your e-mail by listing four specific dates and times that work for you under the heading of "My availability." This is an opportunity for your professional yet easy-to-work-with nature to come shining through once again. Indicate that if none of these options work for him/her, he/she should send you his/her list of times and you will confirm one. Finally, the last paragraph should always thank the person for his/her time and consideration. Politeness always greatly increases your chances of getting what you want.

When you are about to communicate with a potential hiring manager or someone who is reluctant to return a phone call, you will find much greater success with this two-pronged strategy. Combining the phone and e-mail works because one or the other will be a preferred method of communication, and using both helps you find the right one.

Also, if the person's e-mail is not readily available but you were clever enough to find it, he/she may appreciate your tenacity and resourcefulness. (Once upon a time, a friend suggested that I was basically spamming people by doing this, but the opposite proved to be true. Companies invited me in because of my resourcefulness in finding an e-mail address that was not formally listed.) Finally, it's an opportunity to demonstrate how you follow up on promises when many people do not. This increases your credibility factor. My own experience has found this method to work 96 percent of the time—a testament to how powerful it is. I have received testimonials from clients who, in one final attempt to contact someone, gave this a try, and they were deeply grateful for their success in landing that much-desired appointment.

Stand Out With Standard Mail

Expert salespeople find ways in which to stand out above the crowd. Standard mail is almost a novelty these days due to the time and expense involved. I have always found that a humorous follow-up card or a handwritten thank-you note catches the eye of the person I'm trying to reach. In fact, many have saved my notes and cards. If you do decide to use standard mail you must ensure your note stands out, beginning with the envelope. Attention to detail is another sound strategy used by sales professionals. Purchase commemorative stamps that catch attention (as long as they are professional). The stamp will help make the letter look personal. Use white or cream stock, and hand-write the address using a style other than the standard business style. All of these tactics will have your recipient eagerly opening up the letter to find out what's inside. The underlying message is that you are clever and creative, and you may become the one candidate they want to interview.

Give Away Samples of Your Talent

In your interviews you can give out samples of your work ahead of time, just as Baskin-Robbins does. When executed cleverly, this technique can bring about an interview before there's even an actual job posting. If you are in a creative industry you might wish to show off your creative abilities. For example, my daughter Tanya's initial interview for a marketing manager position went very well, so she decided that she would demonstrate her creativity in her follow-up. As the position was described to her, it was evident that branding strategies for the company was a requirement. So she purchased a cute miniature stuffed cow with an accompanying branding iron. Tanya gave careful consideration to how she would get her special package delivered to the director. She didn't know anyone in the company who could help her, so she asked a friend who has the ability to maneuver his way to any decision-maker. He cheerfully delivered the package to the director of the marketing department. Included with the package there was a note that read, "I know you're looking to beef up your marketing, and I can also help with your branding. Please give me a call!" Her creativity in anticipation of the marketing position worked. Tanya received a call that day with an invitation for a second interview!

Selling Yourself Interviewing Tips:

- Use the friendship approach, even when you are cold-calling.
- Position yourself as trustworthy, credible, and easy to work with.
- Always think of things from the other person's point of view.
- Discern whether the other person is preoccupied or relaxed.
- Listen for what is being said and what is being left unsaid.
- Use more than one method of communication.

- ✍ Avoid telemarketing techniques—never use a script!
- ✍ Begin every communication from the other person's point of view.
- ✍ Demonstrate your creativity in your follow-up mailings.
- ✍ Always make it easy for others to say yes.

Researching and Qualifying
Your Prospects

The Boy Scout motto, "be prepared," applies to every important endeavor in your job search. The activities described in this chapter may sound time-consuming, but the more research you do upfront, the better you will perform on the actual interview. You want to be as efficient and thorough as possible before running off to a variety of interviews. Research all of the contact information you acquire prior to arranging your appointments. Develop a checklist for everything that needs to be researched first. Do you understand each facet of the hiring company's business, or do you need to seek help for clarification?

If you are thinking that this advice doesn't apply to you because you are just applying to be a part-time cook at a hamburger chain, let's consider another possibility: the hiring party may very well see you as an extraordinary candidate and want to groom you for management while he/she is training you to flip those burgers. The more professional you are, the more you will be seen *as* a professional.

As you research and qualify your prospects, you must first determine if

- ✎ the job is of interest;
- ✎ the company meets at least some of your requirements;
- ✎ the salary range will meet your expectations.

Just those few steps alone may eliminate several possibilities. The more qualified you make your prospect list, the more likely you will find a job you truly want. In this way, it's similar to the dating process!

Corporate Contacts

1. Investigate the company's financial standing.

Now that you have a workable list, determine if the company is in good financial standing. It doesn't matter what its Website promises if it is filing for bankruptcy. If the company is publicly traded, find out the past history of its stock. Further investigation will let you see a snapshot of the company's financial outlook for the past several years. Is it moving in an upward or downward trajectory? Is there talk of it merging with another company? If so, will your intended company be the acquiring party or the one being sold? What has its employee growth been like during the past five years?

2. Research management.

If it is a smaller company, read about management and their philosophy of conducting business on the company's Website. You might also check to see where they were educated. In the midst of the worst economic decline the United States has seen since the Great Depression, my colleague Cheryl shared with me that she was able to secure the job of a lifetime. When she described what she did, I had to agree that the opportunity was phenomenal. I asked her how she was able to get the job given the difficulty most businesses are facing. With a grin on her face, Cheryl explained she researched the company Website prior to picking up the phone to call for an appointment. When she noticed that both she and the CEO went to the same university, this gave her the confidence she needed to give him a call. When Cheryl called to introduce herself to Mr. CEO, she let him know that they went to the same university. He said he wasn't in a position to hire her right then and there, but extended a friendly welcome and invited her in for a visit. Because Cheryl knew to build commonality during the conversation, they quickly realized they both came from the same small town in the Midwest and, in fact, knew many of the same people. Mr. CEO was so excited to find someone from his home town, he ended up hiring Cheryl on the spot!

3. Look for the mission statement.

The company mission statement will also provide you with insight as to how the company views its clientele and its approach for conducting business. For you to be happy at the company, this is something you will want to find out about and mention during the interview. With the mission statement fresh in your mind, research articles written by clients to determine if what is written is in sync with what is stated on the Website.

4. Look at other pages on the Website.

The "About Us" page will typically tell you how and why the company was formed. Thus it provides more background understanding and a basis for beginning a conversation. On the "Products and Services" page, review everything the company has to offer. Contemplate how all of their revenue streams work together toward the core business of the company. How will the position you are about to apply for impact company revenue? Where will you fit in the company "machine"?

5. Comb for keywords.

Now that you know the company is financially sound and have discovered interesting information about its partners, read its entire Website carefully and look for embedded keywords. These words identify what is unique to the company and help increase the number of visitors to the Website. They will also tell you what is most important to the company. When you see them repeated either on the same page or on several different pages, you will know to use these words during your introduction and your interview.

A number of years ago, I was selling to Fortune 100 companies, and a particular bank was on my list to call. Upon reviewing its Website, I saw the words "financial soundness" repeated many times. This was my cue for a phone introduction. When I called my contact, I said, "I see from your Website that financial soundness is of great importance to your bank. I represent Fortune XYZ. Do we have enough financial soundness for me to secure an appointment with you?" The woman began laughing and then asked, "How did you know all of this? Of course you can come in!"

The same principle applies to calling your prospects for a job at a particular company. Thoroughly review its Website and all supplementary materials you can find. When you find a commonality, a point of interest, or something newsworthy, you can open with a comment on that item first, and then introduce yourself. When you begin your call with a statement about the company, the other person will be trying to think of a clever answer and thus will be ready to hear your name and the reason for your call. Demonstrating that you know something about their company builds confidence and trust in you right from the start.

6. Read client testimonials.

Do the testimonials appear to be genuine? Did the company solve a problem for its client? Consider whether the testimonials uniformly focus on one area of the company versus the many areas of engagement possible. If they are focused on one area only, this could mean the company is experiencing a challenge with its other services.

7. Find out about positioning.

Are you able to determine how the company is positioning itself against its competition? Where does it excel? Does it do things differently, or is it fairly mainstream? Ask yourself whether you want to be with a mediocre company or one that is highly innovative and successful.

Vertical Marketing

Once you find a company that appeals to you, you should start thinking about becoming an industry expert. Every industry develops its own jargon, words that most people don't use (and probably don't understand). You should become proficient in this jargon and able to use it easily in conversation. Also, by researching other players in the industry, you will quickly become one of them by the time you interview. This will make you appear highly credible compared to the other interviewers. To develop your vertical marketing expertise, ask for informational interviews with competitive companies within the same industry. Try to connect with someone who is willing to share inside information with you.

Informational interviews

The purpose of an informational interview is to investigate and learn about an industry in order to determine if it's where you want to be, and to learn about the current challenges within that industry. By the time you have your interview appointment, you will have had time to prepare pertinent questions as to how the company is handling these difficulties and moving beyond them. You will also start to become more familiar with the vocabulary of the industry. When you use industry jargon during your interviews, you will look like an insider who is easy to train, which will move you up the ladder to the short list of desired candidates.

Fewer people are working now that the economy is struggling. As a result, the people who *are* employed are often doing the work of at least two employees, so they may not have a lot of time to grant for an informational interview. Be aware of this and be *very* considerate of their time. The next best thing to do is to try to reach someone on the phone to more quickly gain the inside information you need. My own example doesn't pertain to an interview, but it illustrates the same principles.

The first job I landed in the high-tech world required that I sell advertising on financial Websites. There was no training, and I had no clue how to sell anything online. It was all brand-new. My targets were large advertising companies. I called the marketing director of one of the companies, introduced myself, and asked if she would be willing to answer a question. When I received the green light, I let her know that while I was known for excellent customer service, I was unfamiliar with the decision-making process that advertising companies used to determine if a Website was worthy of expenditures on behalf of their clients.

The director's response surprised me. She said, "You are the first person to ever ask. I will be thrilled to tell you everything!" I was given a long list of requirements of what was needed by agencies in order for them to consider advertising on our Website. Being the sales pro that I am, I asked her if she would consider our site on behalf of her clients if I were able to give her that information. Her answer was "Absolutely!" A sale was made within 48 hours. I then took everything I learned from that conversation and approached the directors of marketing at other advertising companies. The appointments increased, as did the revenue.

You could approach your calls the same way. However, instead of asking how they purchase, for example, you might let them know about your interest in the industry and ask how they choose their candidates for hiring. When you approach others with respect and appreciation for their time, and you ask for help, more often than not that help will be provided. Once again, the principle of relationship building will help you get what you want.

Individual Contacts

Networking etiquette continues well after the event is over. You must follow up with everyone you meet. Your connections and budding relationships will die if you fail to do this. Even if it was just an exchange of pleasantries, send an e-mail stating that you enjoyed meeting them and that you wish them the best. If someone tells you to call or e-mail because they may have a lead, make sure you do so in the manner he or she suggests, whether via e-mail or phone.

Most people fall down on the follow-up!

Remember that you are selling yourself to get the interview *and* the job. Most people fall down on follow-up because of the negative voices in their heads. They convince themselves that the other person was just being nice, doesn't really have a lead, and/or will be bothered by their call. Some people may make a call or two, but then quickly become discouraged when the first couple of attempts yield no results and no returned calls. It is true that some people do not have the gumption to tell you the truth (that they don't have any leads and can't help you). Instead, they tell you to give them a call. Then you try in vain to reach them, but, of course, they don't have the good manners to get back to you. I agree that this process can be very frustrating and can feel like a complete waste of time. However, there is good news: the people wasting your time are most likely wasting the time of others, too. They are building a very bad brand for themselves and will, more than likely, eliminate themselves from the competition. Think also about the sales credo, "The more rejections you receive, the closer you get to the yes you are seeking." Hopefully this will provide you with the motivation to keep on pursuing all avenues.

To this end, it may help if you make the decision to not take any of it personally. During difficult economic times, people can sometimes act strangely. The only safe assumption to make is that almost everyone is experiencing some challenging circumstance, such as concern about paying bills, stress regarding protracted unemployment and/or where the next job is coming from, or just general worry about the future. That said, you may find that a small percentage of your new acquaintances will not only have good information, but will be willing to get together with you over a cup of coffee. It can be highly motivating to arrange a couple of these meetings each month. By taking the time to meet someone in this casual setting, you are creating an environment that is conducive for good conversation. Between the two of you, you might come up with some new and clever ideas. Should your newfound friend be employed or have a lead for you at another company, be certain to not only take the contact information, but also to ask industry-related questions. Ask your friend to tell you all he/she knows. Be prepared with a pad of paper and a pen so you can take notes.

Your all-time best route is to follow up on *every single lead*, no matter what the end result may be. Determination, a plan of action, and follow-up is what will get you the interview—and the job!

Selling Yourself Interviewing Tips:

- ✎ Be prepared—do your homework prior to the interview.
- ✎ Become a vertical marketing expert—familiarize yourself with industry jargon, industry players, and insider information.
- ✎ Research management, financials, positioning, and clientele.
- ✎ Read the company Website in its entirety.
- ✎ Comb the Website for keywords and commonalities.
- ✎ Ask for introductions.

- ↳ Go on informational interviews.
- ↳ Follow up with everyone you meet.
- ↳ Approach everyone as a potential friend.
- ↳ Express appreciation for everyone's help and time.
- ↳ Weed out what you don't want and use your time wisely!

Relationship-Building

One of my better sales managers once told me that selling is like a football game. This analogy is particularly true of interviews. During the course of your job search, you may feel as though you are being blocked and even tackled when all you really wanted was to run past the goal line for a touchdown. Have you ever read about or actually watched an athlete in training? They become utterly focused on exactly what they need to do to win. This applies whether they are involved in an individual or a team sport. Any areas of weakness are worked on day and night until every aspect of their training is firing on all cylinders and their standard of perfection is satisfied. They are true champions. Everything you do in life—including your job search—should be pursued with the same commitment to excellence.

Think for a moment what would happen if athletes did not continually work to perfect their game. Would their fans continue to support them, or would the crowds fade away? There is an underlying contract with their fans that they will do everything possible to produce a winning game. This is the identical process that should be used when you interview. When you honor *your* underlying contract for excellence, not only will you be a champion but you will also build your personal support system, your "fan club," to cheer you on to further success. The best thing you can do prior to an interview is to get into the mindset of the person who is about to interview you. You know you are a champion in your area of expertise, but the real question is how you can convert the person interviewing you into a fan so that he or she will give you a strong recommendation to the final decision-maker. This should be your end goal for the interview. There are several ways to do this.

First, begin every communication from the other person's point of view. For example, let's say you are a chef and wish to work at a five-star restaurant. A major mistake would be to immediately launch into your talents and knack for creating specialty meals. A better approach would be to first find out why there is an opening. Did another chef quit, or did he or she fail to live up to expectations and get fired? Is the loyal clientele dwindling in numbers? Are they looking for new menu ideas or specialty events? Before you launch into a description of your talents, it is up to you to play consultant and detective all at the same time to find out in detail why you are sitting in that interview chair and what problems they are trying to fix. Once you know why they are interviewing you, it will be relatively easy to position what you have to offer as the solution to their needs. When you speak to the interests of the other person first, he or she becomes far more interested in you.

Second, avoid telling-selling. Instead, ask questions such as "Have you ever thought about X?" In this manner, you will know whether your next idea will be of interest or whether you should forego that thought and move on to the next one. This will demonstrate your leadership skills as well as your creative side, making you more credible, and hence desirable, as a potential employee. Thoughtful questions and creative answers will increase your chances of getting the job.

Third, demonstrate you are the right fit for their need(s). Focus on how you will bring value to the job and the company. It's up to you to determine what their needs are and demonstrate how you will not only fulfill those needs but will also add new value. Using the example of the chef on an interview, you could suggest a monthly *prix fixe* dinner menu, a different international theme one Friday each month, or quarterly fundraisers with entertainment tied into the theme of the food served for that meal. The new value consists of the creative ideas you bring to the interview. This tells the interviewer you gave the job—and the company—very serious consideration prior to walking into the interview. It will also speak to the fact you are working hard to build a career and a solid reputation, as opposed to simply being interested in cashing a paycheck every month.

Take a moment to consider 25 people who have similar skills: who will get the job? All other things being equal, the person who is most memorable and likeable—the person who has likely used relationship-building skills—will often win the offer of employment. So, in many cases, the final decision is a subjective one. This is why I offer so much advice here on how to make yourself likeable by building relationships and observing proper etiquette.

Be professional at all times.

Be Prepared

The night before your interview, prepare everything you need to bring to your meeting. Print several copies of your resume on high-quality resume paper to increase the chances of a favorable first impression. Review the contents of your resume one last time to ensure that you look sharp when the interviewer asks you about a specific point. Recap in your mind why you think you should be offered the job. How will your skills address the company's needs? Do you have supporting documentation that will prove you have the required skills and dedication to help the company achieve its goals? Become the expert on how you can fill the gap so that the decision-makers recognize their urgent need to have you on staff. Finally, get a good night's sleep and manage your time the day of the interview so that you don't have to rush. One of the best impressions you can make is to walk in looking relaxed, professional, and confident. This image will help you get noticed, the first step to securing the job.

To prepare for a phone interview, be certain to set aside a quiet and private space for the interview. This will help you avoid potentially embarrassing moments and keep you sounding professional at all times:

> Since Assistant Match is a virtual company, our interviews are over the phone. It never ceases to amaze me when people fail to realize they need to treat a phone interview just as seriously as an in-person interview. If they want to work from home they need to treat it exactly like their office setting. In essence it is a demo for what they do. We have had people eating during the interview, holding crying babies, speaking near a blaring television or squawking birds. The best is when they say they have a perfectly quiet home working environment without any background noise, and "Polly" is asking for a cracker. That doesn't exactly scream professional work environment to me! (Katie Gutierrez, CEO, Assistant Match)

Create a Lasting Good First Impression

The expression "Don't judge a book by its cover" may sound like good advice, but the reality is that hardly anyone ever follows it. The moment you step into the office you will be creating a lasting impression, so make sure it's a good one. Dress professionally (within your budget) and wear a nice smile. Don't chew gum or wear clothes that have stains on them. Female readers: leave your purse in the car. Bring a briefcase or small binder with a notepad instead, to hold what you need for the meeting. Everyone, male or female, should bring a small, professionally bound notepad and a quality pen to the interview. If you have business cards, include them in your binder. Arrive at your destination 10 minutes early; this will give you time to get settled and do a little detective work in the lobby (see the following section). Arriving any earlier will send a message that you don't have anything better to do. If you are unable to put your best foot forward, your interviewer will assume that your every-day behavior and demeanor are even worse. As a colleague of mine recounted:

One time I was interviewing a candidate. To begin with she showed up 45 minutes early for the interview. When I told her that she was super early, she nonchalantly told me that she knew. I asked her to go to a local Starbucks but she said she would wait in the lobby. I had scheduled several interviews back to back so she saw all the other candidates coming and going. It was very awkward to have her sitting in the lobby watching me greeting and escorting other candidates in and out of the office. I was very un-comfortable. Finally, it was her turn to interview with me. I took her into a small interviewing room but she was wearing so much perfume that I couldn't stay in there with her. Granted, I am very sensitive to smells. However, it was so much perfume that other people commented on it. Even after she left, you could still smell her perfume in the rather large lobby. When I told her that I couldn't interview her in that small room and had to take her to a larger conference room, she acted surprised and said that she had barely put any on! Needless to say, she did not get the job. (Anna Brambilla)

Always turn off your cell phone before you walk into the office building! If you happen to carry a smart phone that contains your calendar, keep it with you but turn it off. If you are asked what your schedule looks like for an interview with the CEO, you have the green light to turn on your phone or bring out your mini day-timer to set the return appointment. The person asking for your availability will be relieved that you won't need to play phone tag with each other to make it happen, and your ability to respond on the spot will make you look polished and professional.

The job market is highly competitive. Do you have a plan in place for the possibility that you will be asked for a return interview when you already have something else scheduled? How will you handle this? Any perceived awkwardness may dissuade the interviewer from offering you another invitation. It will be difficult to disguise your hesitance when you check your calendar only to find you already have an appointment for the date and time suggested. Familiarize yourself with your calendar and devise a plan ahead of time. If it comes to it, say that you would appreciate an appointment an hour or two earlier or later, but if this is not possible, that you will reschedule your current appointment because you know the job is just perfect for you. This kind of a response lets the interviewer know you are a person of dependability and integrity, that you have leadership capabilities, and that you are very serious about wanting the job. Stating that the position is a perfect fit for your talents will be the icing on the cake!

Avoid the totem pole syndrome

Treat absolutely everyone in the office as if they were the CEO in charge of determining whether or not you will be hired. Make it your priority to treat everyone with equal respect. Some people will talk down to the doorman, the receptionist, and/or the person walking them down the hall-way. They forget that, many times, the "low man on the to-tem pole" may in fact be filling in for an ill employee, may be related to the CEO, or may be an executive him-/herself. In addition, hiring managers often try to find out how you treated their staff in order to gain some insight into how you might work as part of a team. The answer could determine your fate and whether or not you hear "HIRED!"

Before all else, say something nice!

Play Detective

Play detective in the lobby of the company. Do they have awards on display? Are there letters from clients posted on the wall? If so, what do those letters say about the company, and can you use something you read there as a conversation starter? Do they have artwork displayed on the walls? If there are motivational posters with quotes attached, do any of the quotes resonate with you? Companies display these types of things in their lobbies for a reason. These displays are intended to let visitors know what is important to the company and what they are most proud of. By keying in on the significance of each item, you will begin to get a grasp on the company culture and learn to speak its language. The more you sound like an employee (or at least demonstrate a similar way of thinking), the more likely it is that you will hear "HIRED!"

As you step into your interviewer's office, say something nice about the room because it is the person's home away from home. After all, he or she spends most of his/her waking hours there during the week, and most people are proud of their office environment, particularly if they have made it to management status. As you are complimenting the office, extend your arm for a friendly but firm handshake. While you are shaking hands, and before the conversation begins, smile and look the person in the eye. Then, show respect by waiting for an invitation to sit down. This will help set you apart as the candidate of choice. If you hit it off with your interviewer, you will have a lot more leeway in the interview. If not, the results can be disastrous:

When I was recruiting for a high-tech company, I got a lot of attitude from people who had no business being arrogant. One applicant came in to interview. He clearly thought he was much more important and much better qualified to do my job. This fellow barely answered my questions, and when I did ask a question, he would look at me with such disdain like he couldn't believe that I would ask such a stupid question. The straw that broke the camel's back was how he shook my hand. Every time I shook his hand, he would twist his wrist so that his hand was on top. It was so clearly a power move that it instantly turned me off and we did not hire him. (Anna Brambilla)

If the office does not stand out in any special way, the next best thing to do is to take a quick look around and see if you can spot something that indicates a commonality between you and the interviewer. Try to establish common ground from the beginning and make your opening remarks within that framework. For example, many people are proud of their alma mater. If your interviewer has a diploma or other memento of his/her school displayed, you could comment on the fine reputations of its sports teams—unless you attended there, too, in which case you will have a lot to talk about! Look also for family photos, pictures of pets, interesting book titles, antique furniture, beautiful carpets, the view from the window, autographs from celebrities, travel photos, or clues of hobbies. Any of these will help you begin the conversation naturally and easily. Whatever you do and say, however, make sure it's genuine. When you remain honest and true to yourself, you stand a far better chance of moving through the hurdles of the interviewing process.

Years ago, during a sales call, I had a meeting with a gentleman I'll call Dan, who worked for the City of Santa Clara. Quickly taking a scan of his office, I could see that we probably didn't have anything in common. However, Dan had a picture of a horse on his desk. I asked him, "What is the name of your horse?" Dan was delighted I had asked and launched into a 20-minute monologue of how he owned a farm in the Midwest and planned to retire there at the first opportunity. He had a far-off look on his face as he envisioned his retirement. When Dan came back to conversation at hand, he was relaxed and happy to speak with me. From that day forward I enjoyed a lucrative relationship with his departments. This is a great example of how a nice remark can have a positive and long-lasting effect.

Speak in Threes

It is very tempting to answer typical interview questions with snappy comebacks to demonstrate your cleverness. However, the best approach is to provide three concise and articulate points that relate directly back to the job posting and that show that you are the perfect candidate. These points are easily remembered and will provide a framework for a well-rounded answer. Answering this way will also show that you are able to organize your thoughts and speak concisely, clearly, and persuasively. Again, this can set you apart from your competition.

Problem-solution-result (PSR)

Companies typically want employees who are great at solving problems; thus, the behavioral interview question was born. It aims to uncover how you deal with challenging situations and whether you can produce results in adverse situations. For example, if you are asked "Tell me about a time when you had a conflict with a coworker (or customer, or boss)," this is your cue to use the PSR method. In this, you will:

- ✎ Briefly outline the **problem** to provide background for the story;

- ✎ Describe your **solution** (what you did to resolve it);

- ✎ Finish with the impressive **result** (quantified, if possible).

The mistake people often make is that they either provide too much information or they fail to mention the final result. Consider the following example of PSR used on an interview at a company that placed a great deal of emphasis on customer service:

Problem: "A customer called in to complain that the foreign language tapes he had ordered were not working for him and so he wanted to return them. He had spent $600."

Solution: "I spent time asking questions about how he used the tapes and listened closely to his answers. After he had had enough time to vent, I told him that I had several suggestions for him that would make him successful in learning French. He had never tried to learn a foreign language before and I wanted to give him several options that would work with his learning preferences. I also extended his money-back guarantee window by another four weeks to give him time to try my suggestions."

Result: "He ended up keeping the tapes and I had thus saved the company $600 and turned an unhappy customer into a happy one who was likely to recommend our products to other people."

Address potential issues before they do

Many of us have something that occurred in our past that could be perceived as a liability. Some examples are: a large gap on your resume because you took several years off to take care of your family; a health issue; a period in your life when you job-hopped a lot; or a disability. If you feel that the interviewer might be wondering about the unspoken issue, take the initiative and be the first to bring it up. This will help you get past it and move the conversation back to the matter at hand. Treat the delicate issue as if it were a football and you were running with it, determined to avoid tackles, with your eye on reaching the goal line to score a touchdown.

Bring attention to physical challenges and move on!

Radio show host and disability advocate Pauline Aughe states:

As a person with a disability, interviews can be very unpredictable. Once I enter an interview, I'm more concerned with the interviewer's comfort level than I am with my performance. Unless the interviewer is comfortable, he/she will not really hear what I am saying. My disability is like the big pink elephant in the room and until it is acknowledged in relation to my ability to do the job, it can be a stifling and deadly interviewing process. During my first interview out of college with a well-known company, it was completely up to me to turn the interview around. As soon as we sat down, I could immediately sense the uneasiness of the interviewer based on her body language and the questions she was asking and those she was hesitant to ask. She asked me the typical, "Tell me about yourself," but not once did she qualify my skills as a graduate of a reputable university with two internships under my belt. She never once asked, "Can you type since there is a lot of data entry involved with this job?" I knew she couldn't really take an interest in me because she was impaired by her fear of saying something incorrect. Slowly, I got her to look at me as a viable candidate by volunteering my experiences as a college student and an intern for other companies. Soon, she began to ask me the appropriate questions such as, "What are your strengths," "What makes you qualified to do this job," and "How will you get to work?" I passed that round and moved on. Everyone needs to be confident when walking into an interview, but my approach must always be a step better than that of everyone else. I need to get people to see past my disability through to my ability to be a successful and contributing member of any company or team.

Overcoming Hurdles

In sales there are three hurdles each salesperson must overcome, and it is no different in the interviewing process. The three hurdles are:

- ♮ Avoidance or B.S. syndrome
- ♮ Objections
- ♮ Competition

After the small talk and niceties, you will want to prepare for these hurdles. Start off by asking the interviewer what attracted his/her attention to your resume. His/her answer will tell you what is most important to the company. This is *the single most important* question that can put you in the lead for getting the job. This is because you will now know exactly what to zero in on to increase their interest in you. This question also eliminates the avoidance or B.S. syndrome and quickly gets the conversation moving along in the right direction. Equally important, the question will start the conversation from the other person's point of view. Because the question is direct, you will gain immediate insight as to what is important to the company and thus eliminate most objections. And finally, it will put you ahead of the competition, simply because most people don't know to do this! Let's take a look at an example job opening to fully understand how this works.

If you are applying to, say, a prestigious architectural firm and you are fresh out of college, it takes gumption on your part to approach the firm. The interviewer may tell you that the company is impressed that you took the risk to ask them for an interview, because your risk-taking may well translate into taking risk on new designs for homes and office buildings. A girl I know named Jesse did something similar. She graduated from architectural school and applied to a highly recognized company in an upscale community that also happened to be her hometown. During college vacation, Jesse visited family and friends who still lived there. She remained current with the trends there in remodeling and new construction, as well as what the community desired most.

Although the interviewer clearly had his doubts when Jesse first sat down, she began to address them right away by uncovering what the hiring company was seeking in an employee. She then proceeded to present her carefully thought-out ideas as to what she would bring to the firm and to their client roster. Jesse also indicated that because she grew up in the town, she very likely would be able to bring new local clients to the firm. The firm recognized she was a natural fit for their clientele, and clearly loved the idea that she could bring in new clients. Jesse almost instantly heard "HIRED!"

Your skill set only gets you in the door.

Your skill set will get you in the door, but finding out what the employer is looking for can help you overcome those inevitable hurdles and smooth out the rest of the interview process. Most of all, it makes you look intelligent and easy to work with—important components for getting hired. Another example: If you are a salesperson on an interview and you find out that the company is searching for top performers because their sales are low, this will be your clue to go into detail of how you turned around a previously dead account and brought in the entire campus as a client.

It is surprising how many people neglect to put energy and effort into preparing for an interview because it's "just a conversation." Most candidates assume they will be hired because they have all the skills outlined in the job requisite. They fail to notice that the right skill set is a minimum requirement. In fact, the way you present yourself in person and your chemistry with the interviewer are the qualifiers that will most likely determine whether you will be offered the position. Following are a few examples of this truth in action:

In the dot-com heyday a client of mine was called in to an interview, on a Saturday with 30 minutes notice, for a music software engineering position. He had done his homework and knew that the founders of this startup were extremely casual. He conducted the interview wearing shorts and a tank top, with his feet dangling in the pool. He got the job!

—Christine LeMay, career consultant

The people I remember the most are those that come prepared. If you are interviewing for a product-marketing job, bring samples and examples. If it's an advertising or graphic design job, bring a portfolio. Granted, not all jobs lend themselves to creating a portfolio. However, at the very least, bring stories or think of examples of what you have done in the past that's relevant.

—Anna Brambilla, hiring manager

I had to drive 45 miles to an interview so I allowed plenty of time in case of any unforeseen delay. It was only five miles away, but frustration grew as I sat at a highway construction site for over an hour. I was quite late, hot, tired, upset, and wanted to be anywhere but at the interview. One of the male interviewers recognized me as I entered the room. He remembered back to an earlier day when we used to share hotel rooms to save expenses. Seeing that I was quite flustered, he announced to the committee that in fairness to all, he should confess that we once had slept together. That crack broke up both the committee and me. I relaxed and got the job.

—T. Roth

Overcome objections with a smile

It's all well and good to talk about relationship-building and creating rapport, but what if an initially pleasant exchange takes a turn for the worse? What if what you thought would be a pleasant conversation turns into something quite different? Sometimes, ridiculous or even offensive questions will be hurled at you to see how you respond. How you dance this dance with the interviewer will determine the outcome, for better or for worse. Most people freeze, start to mumble, or just kill the interview at this point. A better approach if you are caught off guard by an uncomfortable question is to ask why they are asking that question. Tell them you need clarification in order to be able to give them the answers they need. Asking for reasons and clarification will help you further the sales cycle. When you know the reason behind the question, you will have a much easier time answering. The other benefit of responding this way is that it buys you a little extra time to compose yourself so that you may provide an intelligent answer.

Difficult and insulting questions are asked for any number of reasons. Sometimes they're asked to see how you work under pressure. Sometimes it's a way of getting a sense of your communication skills to find out if you are a good fit, and if so, where they should place you. Sometimes it's even used as a negotiation tactic—if you don't answer well, they can use that as a reason to offer you less. You may wish to consult with a career coach to provide you with insight and practice tips for answering the latest hot-button questions. Every few years the questions change to keep up with the times. If I had just one bad interview, it would be well worth it for me to pay someone for some coaching to avoid another bad experience.

Here are some more typical problematic questions an interviewer will ask you, followed by some general guidance and a few of my favorite answers. In each example, you can see that you need a starting point so that you can reply appropriately and further pique their interest. My answers have worked well for me, but only use what comes naturally to you. Your authenticity is what will ultimately sell you.

- ᜑ **"Tell me about yourself"** (not really a question, but it demands an answer nonetheless). My style is to use humor, so I respond by asking, "There is so much to tell, where would you like me to begin?" Another possible response is, "Are you more interested in the personal side or the business side?"

🐾 **"Why are you looking for a job?"** Always maintain a positive picture of why you are seeking a new job. Even if you are desperate for work, don't let on. Rather than feeling empathy, interviewers might be turned off. You need to be honest in your reply, but couch it in terms that are easy to relate to, such as, "I wish to be more of a team player by contributing my talent to projects that will make a difference for the company."

🐾 **"Why is there a gap in your resume?"** If it is due to a health reason, address that in a very general way while assuring the interviewer that there is no possibility for a recurrence or relapse. Once again, keep the interviewer's perspective in mind. Be honest, but "spin" your explanation in a positive light so that it will be more readily accepted. If you were part of a downsizing, say so. If there were others, let the interviewer know how many. If you are concerned that the interviewer will find out why you were fired from your previous job, "off the record," your best strategy is to take the offense and state the fact up front. Prepare your explanation ahead of time as to why you were fired. Don't even mention the words "personality conflict." Instead, focus on the fact you had a difference of opinion about the direction of the company or department, and then turn the conversation to how you excelled at previous jobs.

No matter what you are asked, keep your answer short and simple, and follow up by asking the interviewer if he/she has any questions or concerns about what you just shared. This is another buy-in question to find if they are okay with you as a candidate. When they say no, you should be back on track again for continuing.

Bridge your answers

"Bridging" is a way of positioning your words to sound attractive to the interviewer. The idea is to move away from a defensive stance and toward an "offensive" one. This is another tactic for turning potential objections into acceptance. Your answers must be truthful yet well-positioned to build your relationship with the interviewer. Following are some examples of how to bridge your answers:

- ✍ **What is your biggest weakness?** Offer an answer that provides the negative flip side of an otherwise positive attribute, and make sure it ends on a positive note. For example: "I'm a perfectionist. What this means is I will spend more time than most on a project. However, I always meet the deadline even if I have to work extra hours. The good news is I always over-deliver on expectations!" This exemplifies how an objection may easily be turned into a huge positive.

- ✍ **What are your strengths?** This applies directly to your prioritized list of attributes and desires for your next job. This is where you need to bridge the gap between your strengths and what the company is looking for. Describe your strengths in terms of how you answer some of the requirements listed in the job description. Speak to what you excel in, why you enjoy it, and where you plan to take those skills. Most of all, try to make those skills align with what the company is seeking. Remember to use those keywords and phrases found on their Website as we discussed in previous chapters.

↬ **Why should I hire you?** The specifics will depend on what field you are in, but you might reply with something like, "It must be costing you a lot to take attention away from your own work to interview candidates. How much is that process costing the company? By hiring me now, you will be able to return to the work you truly enjoy doing and know that the hole in your organization will now be properly filled. Does this sound like something that would be of help to you?" This reply shows consideration for the interviewer's enjoyment as well as for the company financials, and offers a trial close to test the waters once again to determine if you are a candidate in the running.

If you are asked a crazy question, smile, take a deep breath, and answer as best you can. Once again, you need to reflect upon your list and decide what is most important to you. The more closely you can match your personality with that of the people about to hire you, the better off you will be. In any event, be prepared for anything!

Get the Facts First

If you are asked upfront what your salary expectations/ requirements are, *do not* negotiate here. This is part of your research prior to the interview. Even if you have a range in mind, you might reply, "There are so many factors involved with accepting this position that I would have to see the entire package in order to offer a fair expectation." If you were instead to offer an immediate reply with the amount you want, you stand the chance of asking for too little—or too much. If you ask too little, the underlying message is you lack confidence in yourself, but if you ask for too much, you might price yourself out of the running.

The company may have plans to offer a salary or overall package that you never envisioned. By standing your ground, you will have more room to negotiate later. At the same time, when you decline to give a number, it demonstrates your value. It shows that you value yourself and won't leap at just any offer. This will make you appear more desirable. Many salespeople sell their products and services at the lowest price possible just to say they got a sale even though they do not make any money from it. Wiser salespeople ask their prospects up front if they are more interested in service or price. When the soon-to-be client says "service," the salesperson knows he/she can hold his/her price at a higher level. Similarly, you are selling yourself and your services to the hiring company. By waiting until you get all of the facts, you will show your worth and hence be able to sell your services at a higher value. It can also help you command a better offer than the company originally intended. You might ask if the company has a budgeted range to offer candidates, and if so, what that range is. The question demonstrates your willingness to work with the company but doesn't commit you to a number. The more information you have on the front end, the better equipped you will be for negotiating after the offer.

Know the reasons for "no."

Before you leave the premises, make certain you know what the next steps are. If you like what you have heard, confirm the follow-up procedure. This is not a time to be shy! It's important to find out precisely what their expectations are and determine the best way for you to follow up.

When sales representatives lose a sale, they will often return to the client and ask why, and what advantage their competitor had over them. This is referred to as a debriefing. On occasion, the debriefing may even save the sale or lead to another sale that was not previously discussed. This same tactic could also work with interviewing.

Receiving a rejection letter is a major blow to the ego for many people, but it happens to the best of us. Often it is delivered with no explanation and with a complete lack of personal touch. For example, John had what he thought was the best interview of his career. He left the premises ecstatic, knowing his skills and interests were a perfect match for the company. There was no doubt in his mind he would be offered the job. Unfortunately, John received a mass e-mail that went out to all of those rejected, stating, "We need to inform you that you were not selected." John was confused, so he asked his friends if it would be okay to call them to find out where he had erred so that he could do better next time.

Career consultants are pretty much divided as to what they think of this technique; some recommend it, and some do not. Some think that as long as you show no ill will but truly want to use the rejection as a learning experience to improve your results the next time around, then by all means, you should ask for a debriefing. However, if they wish to discuss the factors leading to why the other candidate was chosen, you need to make sure you don't become argumentative. The last thing you want to happen is for word get out that you are difficult or combative. Elaborating on this, Linda Stokely said,

> *Most employers are really uncomfortable with this behavior. A better approach is to send a follow-up note (less confrontational) expressing disappointment in not being chosen but thanking them for being considered and asking to be kept in mind should another opening come up. It is important to note that many times the new employee will turn out to be not the right choice, and then you are in a good position to be reconsidered. If a company told the person why they were not chosen, then it would be hard to say "now we think you would be great."*

Should you ever pursue a debriefing after you've been rejected? As with anything, you must decide if doing so aligns with your personality in order to keep your brand intact. My belief is that if you truly believe the job is a perfect fit for you, you have nothing to lose by writing a note to the interviewer indicating that you appreciate all of his/her time spent considering you as a potential candidate. Next, indicate that should anything change, you would welcome the opportunity to once again interview because you firmly believe that you would be a very good fit for the company. It is often said that people who are horrible at interviewing turn out to be excellent employees, whereas some who interview extremely well prove to be awful employees. The latter may provide you with a second opportunity.

No matter what your field is, the most important ingredient in the relationship-building process is, always follow up! When you check in with a friendly tone to ask what's new and to provide your own update, people will take note; most will admire your persistence. This also plays into the philosophy of never giving up and staying focused on the end game. The rules of etiquette and relationship-building must be adhered to every step of the way so that you will hear HIRED!

Selling Yourself Interviewing Tips:

- ✎ Stay focused and honor your contract for excellence.
- ✎ Convert your interviewer into a fan.
- ✎ Begin every communication from the other person's point of view.

- ✍ Demonstrate that you are the right fit for their needs.
- ✍ Understand what the job entails on the front end.
- ✍ Use proper etiquette to boost your interviewing score.
- ✍ Arrive 10 minutes early (but no earlier!).
- ✍ Treat everyone equally.
- ✍ Recognize the value you bring to the company.
- ✍ Play detective to help build the relationship.
- ✍ Speak in threes and use PSR to overcome hurdles.
- ✍ Get all the facts before you commit.
- ✍ Know the reason for "no."
- ✍ Always remain true to yourself and your brand.

Relationship-Selling

You will read very specific selling strategies in this chapter to apply to your interview, but you must first decide if these techniques are consistent with your personality and whether you will be comfortable implementing them. Authenticity in all you say and do counts the most, especially when you are presenting yourself as a brand.

Neuro Linguistic Programming

Admittedly, my knowledge of NLP is limited. However, the little I do know will help you tune in and deliver a highly targeted conversation. When you become comfortable with this technique, it will almost seem as though you can read the other person's mind at times. This will give you an enormous advantage over the competition. However, my word of caution is to use these tips in moderation so as to avoid being misunderstood.

Visual clues

What you see (rather than what the other person is saying) will give you a clue as to how you should respond. Sometimes this is as easy as observing the look on someone's face. For instance, your interviewer may look downcast as he/she recalls how he/she was verbally chastised by management. Perhaps department heads were beaten up because their staff did not boost revenue. This is your clue to say, "I can **see** by the look on your face that my idea for improvement may be of interest." If you receive an affirmative answer, you can then ask what his or her plan is for the coming year for improvement. When he/she finishes (and at this point know that they are confiding in you), it will be your turn to speak. Share a story from your work history that echoes the hiring company's present difficulties, and make sure you demonstrate that you were able to contribute to the solution.

Tone of voice

An interviewer's tone of voice can also provide clues as to what his/her real concerns are. It may become hushed, lower, or shaky when he/she is speaking about a difficult or uncomfortable subject—for example, perhaps the company no longer has a creative think tank, and this is negatively affecting the department's morale. You can respond by saying, "I **hear** regret in your voice that creativity is not as sharp as it once was. How do you plan to address this?" Watching facial expressions and body language can give you a window into what the interviewer is thinking. By picking up on these clues, you will learn far more than the other candidates vying for the same position who are not in tune with this process. Other than salespeople, not many other people have access to this information. Use it to your advantage!

Kinesthetic (touch)

A smaller portion of the population tends to be kinesthetic. People like this tend to use terms and phrases such as "I'm touched," "I felt," or "It just didn't feel right." If this is the case with your interviewer, respond accordingly: "I **feel** your discomfort with the employee gap/pay cuts/downsizing and will gladly put my talents to good use!"

Body language

Watch the other person's body language for clues as to how your information is being received. Make certain he or she is paying equal attention to yours, as well. Once upon a time, I had the unfortunate experience of interviewing with a sales manager who thought he was too important to listen to me as I tried to carry on a conversation. Instead, he chose to clean his fingernails with one of his keys. His obvious disinterest was very disturbing, so I quickly ended the conversation and left.

Mirroring

Mirroring is exactly what it sounds like: you reflect back certain aspects of the other person (facial expressions, gestures, tone of voice, inflection, and so on) as if he or she were looking into a mirror. In a sense, you "become" that person. Use caution, however: Depending on how adept you are at this, it can either make you look manipulative or (ideally) make the other person very comfortable with you. As the saying goes, people buy from people they like, and people who are comfortable with you tend to like you. You can also mirror someone's vocabulary. Most people tend to use certain words over and over again in their conversations. Should you notice this during an interview, consider using one or two of those words once or twice when you speak. The occasional mirroring will help you build commonality and rapport.

Direct Communication

After the interviewer has finished the initial introduction to the company and the position, it is your turn to reply. Speak directly to the points the interviewer made. Avoidance is the strategy of your competitors; your strategy is to avoid nothing. Meet every hurdle, challenge, and objection with a smile and speak directly to what is being said or asked of you. Do your best to look the other person in the eye as you communicate with each other. The tactic of observing and listening as you interact will fuel the conversation and encourage the hiring party to reveal more.

If, while you are speaking, you see an eyebrow raised, arms folded, or a chair abruptly pushed back, stop mid-sentence and ask if the interviewer has a question. If this happens, it generally means that you said something that was misunderstood or disagreed with. If you do not immediately stop to check for questions, the interviewer might focus on that one questionable bit of information for the rest of the conversation, and all of your credibility will be lost. It is your responsibility to make certain that does not happen. When you immediately respond to a misunderstanding or question and clarify what you mean, you will come across as being sharp, insightful, and easy to work with. Your communication skills (as well as your sense of responsibility and willingness to go back and fix something that isn't right) will reveal you as a team player. It is the same process as discussed in the previous chapter: problem-solution-results.

It is also very likely that your competition will not know the proper way of directly addressing these subtle cues; indeed, they may even miss them altogether. Even salespeople, who are trained on these matters, often fail to use these strategies to their advantage. Through the years, I have asked job seekers if they know about these cues, and they did not. In my coaching groups, I shared these skills with attendees and it was as if a bright light had suddenly been turned on. Many wrote notes of thanks for sharing my insights on the two-way interview (see the following section), the signals to watch for and the questions to ask. The notes indicated that as soon as they embraced these tactics, the interviewer became friendlier and the process became much easier. Conversely, the interviewers' worry diminished because their questions were answered as they were asked. Being in tune with the person who is interviewing you will alleviate some of the stress and will very likely put you in the lead for the job.

Interview the Interviewer

As the conversation develops, think about what you read in the paper and online about the industry. What are the challenges within the industry and how are those challenges affecting the hiring company? Discuss these challenges with the person interviewing you. He or she will be impressed you gave the situation so much thought and may wish to know more. It is quite possible that the interviewer will open up to you about the company's specific challenges. If you can position yourself as a confidante in this regard, he or she may be more willing to let you know about the specific kind of help the company truly needs. The deeper your conversation develops on various topics and the more you are able to speak on a peer-to-peer basis, the greater your credibility will be. The best strategy is to get your interviewer to reveal as many problems as possible by asking questions. This technique will help build a bond between the two of you and establish common ground. Again, this can build a case for you to be chosen over your competitors.

Be direct when you're asking these questions. Remember, you need to assess whether or not you really want to work at this company. Therefore, the interview must become a two-way street. You need to remember to interview the interviewer.

Most people interview as if they were on a one-way street. Their desperation for a job leads to a certain timidity, and they merely answer the interviewer's questions. Instead of being proactive, they fail to show how they have prepared, what they have accomplished, or how they can benefit the company. They fail to ascertain the company's needs and demonstrate how only they can fulfill them. There is no give and take in the conversation. The end result is that the interviewer cannot get a feel for who they really are. Instead of hearing "You're hired!" on their way out of the interview, they hear "Next!" You, however, now have the tools to avoid this. If you want a job where you simply do the work and collect a paycheck without having to interact with anyone, a more passive style of interviewing may work for you. But if you want a job where you will have a say in what's going on, it is best to interview as if you are on a two-way street—because you are!

An easy way to find that two-way street is to establish "buy-ins," or mini-agreements you establish throughout the conversation. To make a sale, you must establish three to five buy-ins and three to five needs. One of the best ways to establish a buy-in is to ask, "Is this what you are seeking?" after you have answered a question. When you get to "yes," you have a buy-in. If you interview this way, you will be noticed and remembered. It demonstrates you are not afraid to take charge, can think independently, and want to fully understand every situation so that you can make an informed decision. This is the type of employee most companies seek (or should seek). When you are able to speak as an equal during the conversation and ask difficult questions of the interviewer, just as he/she does of you, you are more likely to be seen as the expert the company is seeking. Companies interview candidates because they need help, and the best help comes from leaders or those who are team players. Demonstrating you can rise to the occasion and work as an equal will give you a real edge.

Once you've established what the company's challenges and needs are, create opportunity by asking these types of questions:

- What do you see as solutions for these challenges?
- What changes will need to be made?
- How will your team help you?
- What attributes are you seeking in the person who will be filling this role?
- Can you prioritize the qualifications you desire?
- How will you make the final determination as to who best meets your criteria?

Once you are able to get the interviewer to tell you exactly what the company is looking for, you can more easily demonstrate how you meet its requirements. Just as important, your answers will be targeted to the company's desires. Essentially, both parties must have their questions answered fully in order to move to the next step in the interview process.

Selling Yourself Requires Thought

Make sure you think ahead about how your questions will come across to the person conducting the interview. You need to be certain your questions are on target for getting the job. When you stray too far from the subject at hand, you are more likely to be misunderstood—or even worse, put off the interviewer. As a forewarning, there are a few questions that should be off-limits:

- ✍ Are there people I should avoid if I take this job?
- ✍ Is it okay if I take a power nap after lunch?
- ✍ How much money are you offering?
- ✍ May I postpone the drug test?

Ed, a hiring manager, shares the following story about the most peculiar question he was ever asked by a candidate:

I was all set to hire this fellow. He had all of the skills and ambition I was seeking until he asked the following question: "Are there a lot of banks in town and which is the closest one?" I asked the candidate why the number of banks was important to him. He never got to specifics but indicated he had a strong need to be near a good number of banks. His question and answer were both peculiar and they almost made me nervous. I couldn't help but wonder if he were a bank robber at night! Although he had the right skill set for what we needed, I turned him down for the job.

Now let's examine the kinds of questions you *should* ask throughout the interview:

What are the goals for the department?

The answer will give you an idea of whether the goals of the department are realistic and whether they are something you want to be a part of.

Assuming I'm chosen, what types of goals will you set for me?

Be aware that the answer may not be entirely truthful. However, it will give you at least an indication of what you can expect. More importantly, phrasing the question in this manner will have the interviewer seeing you as the employee. It provides more of a psychological impact than any real insight for you.

Is it a team environment or would I work solo?

Personally, I would want to know if I were going to be placed in a cubicle by myself, or if collaboration is a major part of the workday. As always, you should know what is important you.

Does the team work with other departments?

If you are a social person, interaction among departments may be very important to you. If not, being closely aligned with only two or three other people, or none at all, may be preferable.

If I were to stay on long-term, what could I expect my career path to look like?

You need to know if the position you are interviewing for and company you are interviewing with has room for career growth. The answer may make a huge difference on whether or not you want to accept. This question is so important that I have stated it twice in this book. Employee turnover, and the additional training that requires, puts an enormous financial burden on a company. Interviewers want to be certain you will not be moving to another company or country in three months. So when you speak to career path, the question automatically removes that concern.

Do *you* plan on being here long-term?

I have heard of instances in which the interviewer quit prior to the new candidate coming on board. If you have created a bond between yourself and the interviewer, it can be a disappointment to find out that the person who was instrumental in hiring you is no longer with the company. You might even feel betrayed and wonder what's next. Hence, you may wish to add this question to your list.

Make sure you ask insightful questions about the company, too:

What is your market share and how do you see it growing?

Ask this question if you were not able to find it in business news. No matter what position you are applying for, you want to know whether or not the company will be around for a few years. You will also want to know about its corporate directives and policies. Not every question will be answered, but you will be able to learn a lot by observing the way they are handled. The more your questions show critical thinking, the more likely you will differentiate yourself from everyone else and be seriously considered for the job.

Does the company have new directives to increase growth?

Not all companies will share this for fear of inside information getting back to its competitors. But some general ideas of strategies for growth should be shared to encourage your continuing interest. The answers will also give you some insight into management. How they approach business—aggressively or conservatively—will be clear. This will help you determine if you agree with their philosophy.

Who else will be making the final decision on the candidate to hire?

This question has two important elements attached to it: first, it begs the question of whether others are involved in the decision-making process; second, it is an indirect way of asking what you can expect as the next step. If you are told that additional people will want to interview you, find out their titles and the approximate time frame for meeting with them. Different departments tend to have their own ways of thinking and doing things, so you will want to do some research if you aren't certain as to what types of questions you should ask of each department head.

Find Out Where You Stand

No matter whom you will be meeting with next, let it be known you welcome the opportunity to meet the other members of the team. You also want to know all of the factors going into the process to determine if you have a serious chance for securing the job. Typical questions to determine where you stand are:

🖐 How many other candidates are you interviewing?

🖐 When do you expect to make a final decision?

🖐 When is the targeted start date?

🖐 What are your top three priorities for a candidate?

When you pose this last question and receive an answer, you can then determine if you are the right candidate. Assuming that you are, you will then know exactly the qualities you need to demonstrate to the interviewer.

Trial Close

Up to this point you have made it through the first hurdle of getting past initial objections. You did this by getting on the same page, leading the conversation, and thinking ahead about what the company desires in its chosen candidate. You now have a big advantage over your competition, but you aren't at the finish line yet. Let's go into a little more detail of how the process of the trial close will eliminate the competition.

When you ask why you were chosen from a large stack of resumes, you begin an honest dialogue about the company's current situation. Let the interviewer speak as long as he or she wants when answering your question. The most important thing you can do is listen. While you are listening, think about your skills and how you can help that person or department get to where it wants to be. It is very important that you ask the interviewer to clarify anything you do not understand. Rather than making you look dumb, it will make you come across as honest and eager to learn. At this point in the game, a smart salesperson would ask, "Given everything we've discussed thus far, is what I am selling what you are looking for?" This is called a trial close. If you do this in an interview—for example, "Given your needs and my skills and experience, would it be safe to say that I am the kind of employee you are looking for?"—you subtly test the waters to see how close they are to making a commitment. A good trial close will keep you on track for getting hired.

Assume the Sale

By now you have most likely spent close to an hour with the interviewer and have a pretty good idea if you want the job or not. Assuming you truly want the job, you need to let that be known without looking overly eager. A good sales technique for this is to assume the sale. When you ask your questions, pose them as if you were already working there. Another strategy is to speak as if you plan to remain there for the long haul. For example: "When I become a member of your staff, what will my goals look like?" "How much interaction will I have with other departments?" "Assuming you love the work I produce, what will the next step in my career look like?" And so on. If humor is your style, then you might put a big smile on your face and ask if they prefer you begin work at 8:00 or 8:30 a.m. on Monday. But this must work with your personality. If not, don't do it.

When you have established a decent relationship with the interviewer and can ask these kinds of assumptive questions, the interviewer will begin picturing you in the position you are applying for. The question about career steps also plants the idea you are planning on staying for a long time. This will add to your credibility factor.

Ask for the Next Step

Once you've let the interviewer know that you are interested, ask what the next steps are and, if possible, get a timeline for when a decision will be made. Before you leave the office, ask one last time if he/she has any questions for you. This might elicit a response such as, "I can't make any promises, but if an offer were forthcoming, when will you be available to begin work?" Know what your answer will be ahead of time. Avoid hesitating, and deliver a succinct message: "I am available to begin in two weeks." And of course, follow this up with a trial close: "Will this work for you?" If you get a yes, chances are the job is yours. If the next step isn't clear, however, you'll need to take the lead with a simple question: "When and how would you like me to follow up? Or you might ask from whom you should expect a call—the interviewer him-/herself or an HR director. You should only ask this if it seems likely that you will receive an offer or be returning for a more in-depth interview with more people.

Before leaving the premises, make certain you have the interviewer's business card so that you have the exact spelling of his or her name and title in order to write a proper thank-you note. As the conversation concludes, take one last quick scan to make sure you have everything that belongs to you. You want to appear organized and professional every step of the way, including on the way out to your car.

Linda Stokely offers the following tips for first-time job seekers as well as more experienced candidates:

List volunteer work and work done for friends or relatives without pay. Definitely do this if it demonstrates skills needed in the job. Offer to work on temporary assignment when a need arises, such as an employee calling in sick or out on vacation. It's a great way for them to see your work habits without making a commitment. It also enables you to be seen as a team player who will pitch in whenever needed. [For more experienced job-seekers:] Retirement is a dirty word; avoid saying you are looking for a company that you can stay with until retirement, even if that date is 10 years away. If the interviewer is clearly younger than you, share experiences where you successfully worked for someone younger than yourself, or perhaps mentored a younger person through volunteer work. Revise descriptions of your previous jobs to ensure that the terms being used are current. For example, if you were director of personnel, that title should be changed to director of human resources. Look at job boards that cater to older workers such as Retireeworkforce.com, Primecb.com, and Retirementjobs.com.

Selling Yourself Interviewing Tips:

🖐 Use NLP and mirroring to build the relationship.

🖐 Address objections directly and truthfully.

🖐 Interview the interviewer to create a two-way street.

🖐 Use buy-ins and assumptive questions to create opportunity.

🖐 Ask why you were chosen to interview.

🖐 Ask insightful questions, listen, and clarify when necessary.

🖐 If you do not understand why a question is being asked, ask for clarification.

🖐 Be true to your beliefs and avoid inconsistencies.

🖐 Trial close to see if you are on track.

🖐 Assume the sale and ask for the next step.

From Objection to Trial Close

When you become proficient at answering difficult questions and responding to objections, you will soon combine several steps of the sales cycle into one. You will be able to take an objection, turn it around, receive a buy-in, and create opportunity with a trial close—all in one fell swoop.

There is a secret formula for doing this. The first step is to agree with the person making the objection! You can then easily answer by turning the question into a positive response, and end by asking a closing question. It may seem difficult to understand why you would want to agree with an objection. But think about it: if you agree with someone who is objecting to what you are saying, you instantly remove the power of the statement and disarm the person making it. It's actually a brilliant maneuver.

The second step in the formula is to turn the situation around and cast it in a more positive light. In all the interviews I have been on, probably 50 percent of the interviews presented the same challenging question. This question was always along the lines of "I like you and would hire you, but you just don't seem to have experience in X." This is exactly the kind of statement that would demand this formula for overcoming objections. You must agree with the objection and then turn it around to a positive. In this case you could say something such as, "You are correct in observing I do not have experience in X. However, I had a similar challenge at my last job," and then go on to describe how you overcame that challenge. This addresses the interviewer's concerns *and* turns the negative into a positive. This type of answer will have the hiring manager jumping for joy! It demonstrates you have courage, confidence, a willingness to do whatever it takes, creativity, and leadership skills. You've just earned yourself a great score in just one answer! Once you've turned the objection around into a positive, you can take it a step further and use your excellent answer to close the sale: "Clearly I work as a company champion and am equally dedicated to my team. Is this the type of work ethic you are seeking?" This is a closing question because the interviewer would be nuts to say, "No, this is not the type of work ethic I am seeking." You have subtly maneuvered him into saying, "Yes, you are exactly what I am after." When you get to "yes," it is your turn to ask, "When would you like me to start?" Again, it takes practice to be able to do this, so look for informational interview opportunities or line up three or four interviews within the same time frame so that you will be ready and humming along at peak performance once the most important one comes along. (I'll cover closing in greater detail in the next chapter.)

Use the Buy-In

Mini buy-ins are crucial to making a sale. This is also true for interviewing. An example of a buy-in question would be "Am I the kind of candidate you were hoping for?" By asking this kind of question, you will know whether or not you are in the running for the job. I've found that interviewers are often taken by surprise at this type of direct question, and they often answer very bluntly and truthfully. At the very least, you will know whether the job is worth pursuing.

Uncover Doubts

Sometimes an interviewer will be too polite to raise any concerns about your candidacy. Therefore, it is best to push the issue and make certain every possible doubt is brought out in the open. This approach will take courage on your part, but it will provide you with the opportunity to address those doubts and put them to rest. As you remove doubt, you can also push for one more mini buy-in that you are qualified. Let's take a look at how this process might play out.

Let's say the interviewer said you have almost every skill for which they were hoping but that there is one concern. You are the mother of two young children. His concern is how you will handle the possibility of having to stay late at the office on occasion. Your answer should offer an explanation of how you will be able to easily accommodate the likelihood of having to stay late. To make sure you have removed the doubt, you should then ask, "Does this satisfy your concern?" You will know immediately from his/her facial expression and body language (remember, use NLP) whether or not he/she is satisfied. When the interviewer finally tells you, "No I don't have any concerns at all," you will know that you are most likely in the running. To know where you stand, the direct approach is always best.

Following are a few more sample questions that will help you uncover objections and move to a trial close:

"Do I appear to be the type of candidate you are seeking?"

Admittedly it takes courage to ask that, but personally I would rather hear a no than waste my time worrying about whether or not I'm in the running for getting hired. No matter what, the interviewer will be impressed with your courage and forthrightness.

"When can I expect to hear back from you?"

This question indicates that you are enthusiastic about the opportunity and have a keen interest in the job. Employers want to hear your enthusiasm; they certainly do not want to hire anyone who is lukewarm about the job! Once again, you are offering a trial close indicating an expectation that you will be seriously considered for the position. This question almost forces the interviewer to be honest about his/her interest and intent.

"I would love the job! When would you like me to start?"

Say this with a smile and only if this is consistent with your style. (A note of caution here: don't ask this if you don't really want the job; you may be surprised by a reply telling you to report in at 8:30 a.m. Monday morning!) Most often, the interviewer will tell you that there are a few other steps that need to be taken first before an offer can be made. This is your cue to ask what those steps are.

The Power of Thank You

Let's return to the interview you just wrapped up. No matter how it was—good, bad, or mediocre—if you truly want to put yourself ahead of the competition, make sure you use the power of thank you. Most people send their thank-you notes via e-mail (if they send one at all). By taking the time to craft a handwritten a note, you demonstrate your thoughtfulness and willingness to go the extra step for others. A handwritten note will also make you memorable. Remember, you are your brand. You want that brand to be noticed and remembered.

Before you leave the interview, be certain you have a business card for each person you meet so that you can write a personal note to everyone involved. Keep a stack of thank-you notes with you at all times, along with a pen, stamps (a commemorative stamp will add that extra creative touch), and return address labels. Keep these items handy because the conversation you just had with the hiring manager will be freshest in your mind right after you leave the interview.

Keep your notes simple. Let them know that you believe the job is a good fit, and state that you believe it would be a good match with your skills and interests. Mention that your desire is to bring new insight to the team to help the department and company grow, too. Make sure you include your phone number underneath your signature to make it easy for them to call you. The quickest way to a sale or a job is to make it very easy for the hiring manager to say yes.

Paint the Picture

Let's assume that all of the above is true: You enjoyed the conversation and liked what was shared in the meeting. You believe wholeheartedly that the position offers a good fit for your talents and interests. To get the job, you must now take the lead in painting a positive picture as if they had already hired you. Again, this is the assumptive approach. You want to mentally paint the picture for them of you in that position. This gives you an added advantage over your competition.

Recap

Recap some highlights of the conversation and reiterate how the job is a perfect fit for your talents. Remind the other person of any commonalities and how they will help the company move forward. Finally, confirm expectations by acknowledging the follow-up steps. This will illustrate your understanding of their goals and willingness to work hard on their behalf. Letting them know when and how you intend to follow up will help you get your other foot in the door. It will also re-confirm that you were listening and will follow through on your promises.

Be memorable

Because a handwritten card is such a rarity these days, sending one will increase the chance that it will be kept on top of the person's desk for a few days. If this is the case, your note—and you—will remain visible and top-of-mind. Given the fact that a mailed thank-you note will take more time to arrive, you should also send a quick thank-you e-mail the moment you get home or back to your office. This gesture will win you extra points for having good manners, punctuality, and thoughtfulness. The e-mail can recap a few additional details, too. If you remind the interviewer once again about the highlights of the conversation, it's more likely that you will stay top-of-mind. Finally, confirm the follow-up steps, and end the e-mail by saying that you look forward to your next meeting and appreciate their time. You'll be well on your way to hearing "HIRED!"

Selling Yourself Interviewing Tips:

- Initially agree with all objections.
- Use objections to state something positive.
- Use buy-ins to see where you stand.
- Uncover hidden doubts and address them.
- When appropriate, embrace the trial close!
- Send a handwritten thank-you note, along with a follow-up e-mail.
- Paint the picture for them.
- Confirm when you will follow up, and follow through.
- Always let your brand guide your approach.

10

Negotiation and the Final Close

The great day has finally arrived—you have been told that the company wants to hire you! All that is left to do is sign the agreement, which will likely entail some negotiation. This is the point at which you should grab your original list of must-haves and review it. Before you sign, ask yourself the following questions:

- ✍ Does this job present almost everything I want?

- ✍ Will the position be good for my career?

- ✍ Are the financial terms acceptable?

- ✍ Is there anything extra I may have forgotten?

Proceed With Caution

Generally speaking, negotiation comes somewhere between your initial interview and your formal acceptance of employment. While you are in the negotiation phase, be certain to ask absolutely every single question that is relevant to the job. Do not ask for any unnecessary information unless you want to come across as annoying. The negotiation phase is still a part of the interviewing process. Nothing is final until all parties have put their signatures on the dotted line.

Check Your Emotions at the Door

What would you do if you had a special occasion (a wedding, an anniversary, a special trip) you had been planning for almost an entire year before you received the offer? How would you handle the dilemma if you had to forego your celebration? This actually happened to me. With a pen in my hand about to sign on the dotted line, I paused. In earnest, I looked up at the hiring manager and said, "Oh, I forgot to tell you. My husband and I are celebrating our 25th anniversary this year. To recognize this milestone, we decided to take a Mediterranean cruise in October. In order for me to accept employment, I will need three weeks of vacation rather than the normal two. Will this be possible?" By the time I was chosen for the job, a lot of time, paperwork, and expense had gone into the process. The hiring manager had worked with me at another company, so he knew I would bring in top-notch clientele for his organization. He was almost drooling at the thought of the anticipated sales I would bring in when I picked up the pen. Surprised at the last minute request, but anticipating the money coming in and not wanting to waste a moment more, he said, "Just sign it and I'll make a notation on the paperwork. Then I'll call corporate to let them know to draw up an amendment. Just sign it." The main point here is to never become attached to what you are getting or what you're giving. Check your emotions at the door and be prepared to walk away. As the saying goes, he who flinches first, loses. Negotiate as if you are willing to walk away, even if deep in your heart you don't want to.

The timing of my request was impeccable. Had I made it ahead of time, most likely it would have been refused. But with the pen in hand, the hiring manager became too anxious. He wanted me on the team so that I could start bringing in more business, which of course would mean more money in his own pocket. Although this was a relatively small issue, I was the only one who secured three weeks of vacation from the company. I did not see him actually initial any paperwork, but because we knew each other, I was confident he would make the terms agreeable to the company.

When you are in negotiations about the variables of your new job, you need to remind the hiring manager of your expertise and everything you are bringing to the table. Once again, recap everything that originally attracted their interest, and paint a picture of what this will look like once your employment is official. You must speak in terms of being a partner with the company in anticipation of getting the required work completed to perfection.

Refine Your List

Few job offers are perfect. If there is anything you feel is missing from your offer, or if there is anything you were hesitant to discuss during the interview process, *now* is the time to put those cards on the table for negotiation. In the early chapters of this book, we talked a great deal about your prioritized list of must-haves. These will be the next stepping stones in your career. A new column should be added to this list for negotiable items. Let's itemize some of them together:

- Salary
- Signing bonus
- Performance reviews
- Possibility for promotion
- Bonuses
- Overtime pay
- Expense account
- Laptop, cell phone, or smart phone services
- Stock options
- Vacation time
- 401K matching program
- Health insurance
- Continuing education
- Second- or third-shift differentials (added income)

🎵 Flextime

🎵 Travel perks

🎵 Relocation

Every job is different, but this will give you some ideas as to what you need to consider prior to accepting a job offer. You might need to take other factors into consideration as you weigh what is most important to you. What is the current economic outlook during your negotiations? In lean times, it will be difficult to gain extra benefits, but in good times, you may be able to get everything you want. Be cognizant of the world around you, and be fair about what you're asking for.

If You Dislike Negotiating...

Use your practice interviews to your advantage

For the people who are timid about asking for more than what they are offered, I suggest the following strategies that will help eliminate stress. The first strategy is actually a natural part of the interviewing process that will free you from extra anxiety. You will most likely interview for several jobs before an offer comes your way. With practice, each interview experience will improve and you will soon be speaking with more and more confidence. Your confidence in the interview is what will sell you to the hiring manager and will help to determine your worth. The ultimate non-negotiating negotiation strategy (if that makes any sense) is to ask for $2,000 more than you did on the previous interview.

For example, if you asked for an annual salary of $48,000 at company #1, at company #2 you will ask for $50,000, and at company #3 you will increase that to $52,000. The fact that you interview better and better as time goes on will increase the likelihood that you will receive the higher salary without ever having to negotiate—and all without any anxiety. It's beautiful!

Plan for multiple opportunities

Perhaps you, like many people, fear negotiating as much as you fear selling. The following beginner's negotiation strategy is designed for you. This laid-back approach will help you secure a higher salary without having to do hardcore and uncomfortable negotiation. A client of mine named Josh shared that when he interviews, he does his best to interview at a number of companies within a small window of time. By doing this, he tries to get two or three job offers at approximately the same time and play them against one another, in order to command the best terms possible. If you choose to do this, however, be careful that you remain diplomatic; otherwise, you may be left with no offer at all. Companies usually allow a couple of weeks for you to accept or decline their offer, so that gives you a reasonable window of opportunity.

Think through all the ramifications

Another caveat is to carefully think out the ramifications of what you're asking for in your negotiation. Once upon a time, I made a huge mistake and failed to do this.

A company was pursuing me, and I knew my worth and was very confident in my ability to get the job done. To my dismay, although I was wined and dined to come over to their side, the offer I received was, at the very least, $10,000 below what it should have been. Because I'm not shy, I let it be known that the amount that was offered was not sufficient. The company tried very hard to create a "take it or leave it" situation. They said that I was lucky to have this offer and that it was the ceiling on what they could offer for my title. I came back with a request that at the very least they give me a $10,000 signing bonus. This request was granted and I agreed to come on board. I was proud of my tenacity and ability to secure the extra money. It wasn't until later that the realization hit me that the $10,000 granted was a one-time gift and would not kick in year after year as the higher salary would have. So this was not a smart negotiation. Examine offers from all angles before saying yes. (On the other hand, there are always exceptions to the rule. This place of business was so poorly managed that the entire sales team quit, one after another, within a two-week period. I quit after only about 6 months, so in this case, the extra $10,000 became a fabulous negotiated sum!)

The Final Close

I learned long ago that there is no magic in closing. It is merely the conclusion of a conversation. If you have followed the order of the selling cycle, you will be just about ready to begin your new career. Once you are handed the document outlining everything you need to authorize, unless something unforeseen happens, the job may be considered yours. It is now your turn to ask about the remaining details concerning your employment:

- ✎ "What time you would you like me to begin on Monday?"
- ✎ "What can I expect my first day/first week?"
- ✎ "Is there anything else you would like me to know about the job, the team, or the company?"

Unless you can think of further necessary questions, conclude with a firm handshake and a big smile. You did it—the job is yours and you are HIRED!

Selling Yourself Interviewing Tips:

- ✎ Review and refine your original list of must-haves; make sure they are included.
- ✎ Proceed with caution.
- ✎ Check your emotions at the door.
- ✎ Act like you're prepared to walk away—even if you aren't!
- ✎ Consider all the ramifications of each negotiable point.
- ✎ Analyze all factors involved in your offer.
- ✎ Remind the hiring party why they chose you in the first place.
- ✎ Always be diplomatic.

- ✎ Wrap up any remaining questions.
- ✎ Conclude with a smile and a handshake—you did it!

HIRED! and Career Planning

Most salespeople focus just on getting the sale. They lose sight of the fact that sales are garnered much more easily through repeat business, referrals, and testimonials. The same holds true for your career. Even though you are now hired and you've begun to establish your career path, the selling process isn't over.

Remember the sales credo that people buy from people they like? Expressions of appreciation for everyone around you, perhaps an occasional lunch with someone who was of immense help in your search, will continue to boost your likeability factor and garner loyalty. You need to continue to sell to your manager, your teammates—indeed, everyone at your company who serves or helps you in any way. Once again, your likeability factor will work in your favor as you ask to work on a coveted project or look for your next promotion.

> *Goals remain at the forefront of the skillful salesperson's thoughts.*

You once had a dream about how your career would take shape, but time, money, and circumstances may have pulled you in a different direction than you had hoped. Now that you are once again gainfully employed, are you able to recall that moment or moments when you were excited about your prospects for the future? Excuses are easy to fall back on—including your need to hold on to every penny in your checking account. Even if this is true, is there something you can do to improve your career path and turn your dream into reality? Put your dream of how you want your career to grow in years to come down on paper. Think about exactly what you would have to accomplish in the next 18 months to be able to say, "I am now on my way to achieving my vision!" Did you notice the excitement that came back into your mind as you began to contemplate how you can actually accomplish your goals? Channel that excitement and bring other people into your inner circle who can help you achieve this even more quickly. (As a side note, negative people are so afraid of failing that they do not want anyone around them to succeed; many will even brazenly attempt to take you down with them. They might even discourage you from trying anything new. The best thing you can do is to avoid these people as much as possible. If you must socialize or work with them, remind yourself that their negative comments only reflect on them and have no bearing on you.)

Set Milestones for Achievement

Career development comes more easily to those who have an open mind about new ideas and strategies. Indeed, this is part of the mindset for success. Excitement about what you do, and being open to new opportunities will attract good things your way. Regardless of the economy, take the time to plan out your career. Do you want to stay at one company in the same position, or climb the career ladder until you retire? Would you rather gain a wider expertise by occasionally changing companies in your field, or by finding complementary positions while you work your way up the corporate ladder? And finally, how do you wish to be remembered by the time you retire? If a biography were written about you, what would you like to say? There is no reason to hold yourself back. With the right planning and the right help from other people, you have the ability to become whatever you wish.

My suggestion is to begin with the end in mind. Shoot beyond what you believe to be possible and write out a plan for how you will achieve it. Make a list of all the major milestones you need to reach to keep you moving toward your end goal in the predetermined period of time. Each week, perhaps on Sunday evening, write out the major tasks you need to complete for the following work week. Promise yourself that you will follow through, then do it!

Documenting Your Accomplishments

Keep track of your accomplishments. This is where documentation is critical. Wherever you are employed, you must keep a record of what you have accomplished in order to sell yourself to your employer for a raise and/or a promotion. This record may also be used for "show and tell" when you interview at the next company. Moreover, it will serve as a reminder to you as to how far you have come in your career path.

One of the best pieces of advice I ever received was to create a monthly document that recaps, in bulleted format, the milestones you have achieved. At the top will be your accomplishments, the middle of the sheet will show projects that need to be continued, and the bottom will contain a list of the projects that did not work out. Be loyal to this one-page document because it will be your best friend for moving forward—and upward—more quickly. When you begin filling this sheet out on a regular basis, you will quickly realize how much you actually accomplish and thus become more confident in your abilities.

For the projects that did not end up well, replace them with projects that might work out down the road. Take the stance big companies take and look at these "failures" as market research. Just by changing your focus and your vocabulary, you will stop yourself from focusing on the negative and feel much better about proceeding with the new plans. This will help you keep going and achieve your goals more quickly.

Develop Your Top 10 List

The top 10 list seems to be everywhere, including movies and sports teams. Your list should include your goals, your criteria for a new job, your prospects for interviewing, and any testimonials and referrals you have from previous jobs. We have all heard the sayings, "Be careful what you wish for" and "What do you really want?" When you itemize your job criteria, consider why they made your list. Do they represent the type of job you truly want? Do they provide you with momentum on the career path you want? Give honest thought to the necessary steps you must take to achieve your goals. Are there some things you would just rather not do? Do you dislike these things so much that they will prevent you from achieving your ultimate goal? Or, will you be able to get the help you need to overcome these challenges? Let me provide an example.

I have been told many times by those in the publishing industry that their clientele will pay them large sums of money to become published authors. But at the moment of truth, when the manuscript is due, the wannabe author will freeze with fear. Even though their fondest dream is to get published, they cannot bring themselves to share their manuscript for fear of criticism. The other fear that would-be authors sometimes have to face is having to promote their book by speaking in front of audiences or hiring public relations people. They expect the book to sell itself. Many would rather let a book sit on the shelf and die than actively promote and market it. They would have saved much time and money had they gotten clear about the facts up front.

Understanding why you want something will give you clarity and greater motivation for moving forward. When you set your goals and record the major things you want to achieve, you need to be crystal clear on the what, the where, the when, and, perhaps most of all, the why. And of course, once you are clear on these things, you will be better able to communicate them to others.

What mini-steps need to be taken for you to know you are making progress, and how will you monitor them? What if setbacks occur? Do you have a plan in place to get around obstacles? By duplicating these exercises for all of your endeavors you will have your own personalized career planning system in place. It will represent an honest introspective and provide you with a much better game plan.

Selling to Management

No matter what kind of job you land, you must treat your team members and management as if they were your clients. Always be available to lend a helping hand and to brainstorm ideas. When your manager makes a request, give it top priority. If you do this consistently, you will soon be granted whatever requests you might make. The moment I implemented these practices, I soon became a company favorite.

Prior to your next review, collect your one-page document listing your achievements and projects. Use it as a basis for justifying a salary increase or a promotion. Most people cannot remember two months back, so when you are able to furnish this document for easy review, you will once again take the spotlight. This is also one of the key elements in making a sale or getting a promotion. Ultimately, in your career, as in your job search, make it easy for the other person to say yes!

Selling Yourself Career Tips:

- ✍ Understand that the selling process isn't over.
- ✍ Consider what you truly want out of your career.
- ✍ Get back in touch with your dreams.
- ✍ Set your milestones for achievement.
- ✍ Create smaller goals in your pursuit of larger ones.
- ✍ Document your accomplishments in order to sell yourself.
- ✍ Change your vocabulary and your mindset.
- ✍ Be clear on the what, where, when, and why of what you what.
- ✍ Make it easy for the other person to say yes!

Questionnaire

*H*ere's a questionnaire for you to personalize the ways in which you plan on leveraging sales techniques to land the job of your dreams. Feel free to photocopy these pages, as your needs and goals will likely change as your career progresses. Review and update your answers regularly, and refer to them before you go on your next interview!

Mindset: *What will you do to get into the right mindset before your next interview? What is your mindset now? What are some ways you can change it if you are feeling tentative or negative?*

_____

_____

_____

_____

_____

_____

_____

Goal setting and planning: *What are your immediate goals for your career? Your long-term ones? Don't be shy here—dare to dream! Ask family members and friends if they can remember what you wanted to be when you grew up—have these goals and dreams changed? If so, do you feel as though you are in control of this process? If not, what can you do to feel more in charge of your career?*

_____

_____

_____

_____

_____

_____

_____

Sales funnel: *How do you plan on expanding your sales funnel (your list of target positions)? List all the non-traditional methods for your search that are available in your area. Don't forget to include seminars, clubs, alumni organizations, and even hobbies as possibilities. Be creative!*

_____

_____

_____

_____

_____

_____

_____

Your brand: *How would you define your brand? If you were a brand of cereal and you had to sell yourself, what words would you use to describe the product (you)? Who would be interested in purchasing you? More realistically, what aspects of your dress, speech, experience, skills, and so on will you need to work on in order to bring them into better alignment with "brand you"?*

_____

_____

_____

_____

_____

_____

_____

Prospecting: *Think about the many ways in which you can prospect for connections. Are you particularly good at, say, networking, but shy away at the idea of a cold call? What steps can you take to address your weaknesses and capitalize on your strengths in these areas?*

_____

_____

_____

_____

_____

_____

_____

Qualifying your prospects: *List each of your target companies here and the information you have found out about them. Are there any red flags that bear further investigation, or which may rule them out as potential employers? Which ones look really good to you? Make sure you remember to follow up with everyone you speak with and meet, and thank them for their time!*

_____

_____

_____

_____

_____

_____

_____

Relationship-building: _List some objections or difficult questions you have encountered in an interview. Did they have to do with your skills, your experience, or something else (perhaps a gap in your resume)? How did you handle them? What will you do better next time? Re-read some of the common questions in this chapter, and write down how you would convert the interviewer into a fan._

_____

_____

_____

_____

_____

_____

_____

Relationship-selling: *Have you ever felt during an interview that the process was just a one-way street? If so, list some questions you can ask next time to "interview the interviewer." Write down a time when you successfully used NLP to uncover an objection or clarify a misunderstanding. Think about how you will apply that to your next interview.*

_____

_____

_____

_____

_____

_____

Objections and trial close: *What is the worst, most blunt objection you have ever heard in your personal life? Your professional life? Now that you know how to turn an objection into something positive (and create a buy-in in the process), write down how you would do that here.*

_____

_____

_____

_____

_____

_____

_____

Negotiation and final close: _Describe a situation in which you felt as though you had "lost" a negotiation. What happened? Did your emotions get out of hand? Write down what you would do differently (use buy-ins, be willing to walk away) this time around._

_____

_____

_____

_____

_____

_____

Your future career trajectory: _Write down some of the ways you will continue to "sell" yourself to potential contacts and to management. This should include your goals (make sure to include mini-goals, too), your criteria for a new job, your prospects for interviewing, your accomplishments, and any testimonials and referrals you have from previous jobs. If you have had what you consider to be failures in the past, write down how you will recast them to reflect your new knowledge of market research._

Hired!

_____

_____

_____

_____

_____

_____

Further Information

In order to improve your skills and advance your career, you must stay in tune with new advancements and seek help as required. Free help is always a great route to take, but on occasion it is wise to consider paying for the help of others. To that end, here are my sales, business, and career book recommendations:

Unlocking the Secrets of the Successful Career Seekers
by Aricia LaFrance

Outsiders on the Inside
by David Couper

Networking: Blueprint for Success
by Betty Daoust

Green Careers for Dummies
by Carol McClelland

*The Power of Charm: How to Win Anyone Over
in Any Situation*
by Brian Tracy and Ron Arden

How to Make Friends and Influence People
by Dale Carnegie

How to Stop Worrying and Start Living
by Dale Carnegie

LEAP! 101 Ways to Grow Your Business
by Stephanie Chandler

*Social Media Means Business: The 30-Day Results Guide to
Twitter, Blogging, Facebook, and LinkedIn*
by Gail Z. Martin

Believe It, Become It!
by Paula Fellingham

If you have questions about the interviewing process, you may wish to consider some of the experts who have contributed to this book as potential resources:

Kristi Frlekin, graphic designer and branding guru:
www.kristifrlekin.com

Christine LeMay, career consultant:
www.balancingyourcareer.com

Rebecca Kieler, corporate career consultant and coach:
www.kielercareerconsulting.com

Linda Stokely, career consultant:
www.stokelycareerconsulting.com

Bethany Brown, partner, The Cadence Group:
www.thecadencegrp.com

Finally, if you are a salesperson and would like private coaching, or if you wish to take advantage of time-tested strategies for incrasing your sales, Smooth Sale, LLC offers a free consultation. You may contact us at (800) 704-1499 or visit our Website at *www.smoothsale.net*. For further insight into relationship-selling strategies that will apply to all areas of your life, please consider my other book, *Nice Girls DO Get the Sale: Relationship Building That Gets Results*. It is available on Amazon at *http://bit.ly/NiceGirlsDOGettheSale*.

My fondest wish is that you find the job you truly desire and hear the word "HIRED!"

Index

About the Author

A vision came to Elinor while she lay on a stretcher with a broken neck at Stanford Hospital. Seeing her life up to that point in the form of a report card, she realized that community service was missing from her life. She recognized a need to give back to communities by using her highly successful corporate sales experience and natural talents.

Elinor began by teaching entrepreneurs how to quickly and easily build their businesses. It had long been evident to Elinor that successful interviewing follows the sales model. Remembering her promise about community service, a portion of her time was always set aside to speak to groups of job seekers on how to sell themselves on interviews. Soon after, requests poured in for her to speak at conferences. When the time was right, Elinor and her associates organized a career and business resource fair for their town. Even though she didn't know a soul in this new location, 200 people were attracted to the event, bringing an outpouring of gratitude for her shared expertise. She quickly realized that it was time to write the book you hold in your hands.

As CEO of Smooth Sale, LLC, Elinor has, through speaking, training, and private coaching, motivated and inspired audiences to achieve their own success. She developed her Smooth Sale training program for corporate teams as well as private coaching. She is viewed as an insightful business growth strategist, and many attribute their success to her strategies. Men and women alike exclaim that her Smooth Sale system is natural and easy to implement, and, most importantly, has greatly increased their revenue stream.

In addition to writing her own blog, Elinor is a frequent guest author for other blogs and magazines. Elinor is a sought-after speaker for conventions and online symposiums, and is a frequent guest on radio shows. Elinor has been interviewed on ABC-TV KGO San Francisco's "View from the Bay," as well as on numerous radio shows. Her first book, *Nice Girls DO Get the Sale*, was featured in *TIME*, was translated into multiple languages, and is still selling strongly worldwide. All of Elinor's programs can be found at *www.smoothsale.net.* Always in the mode of giving, Elinor has also made her podcasts, articles, resource list, and radio shows available for free download on her continually updated "GiftsForYou" Webpage: *http://bit.ly/giftsforyou.*

Connect with Elinor on the following social media sites:
www.linkedin.com
www.twitter.com/smoothsale
www.facebook.com/smoothsale

Also from CAREER PRESS

WINNING JOB INTERVIEWS
Revised Edition
Paul Powers
EAN 978-1601630889

WORK AT HOME NOW
Christine Durst & Michael Haaren
EAN 978-1601630919

HIGHLY EFFECTIVE NETWORKING
Orville Pierson
EAN 978-1601630506

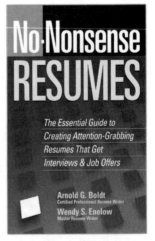

NO-NONSENSE RESUMES
Wendy Enelow & Arnold Boldt
EAN 978-1564149053

To Order Call 1-800-227-3371 or visit CareerPress.com

Also from CAREER PRESS

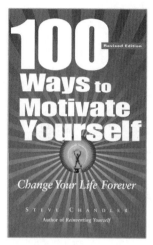

100 Ways to
Motivate Yourself
Revised Edition
Steve Chandler
EAN 978-1564147752

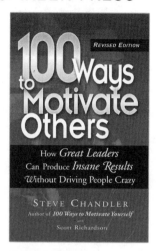

100 Ways to
Motivate Others
Revised Edition
Steve Chandler
EAN 978-1564149923

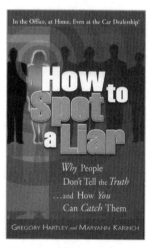

How to Spot A Liar
Gregory Hartley &
Maryann Karinch
EAN 978-1564148407

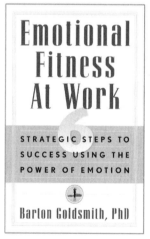

Emotional Fitness at Work
Barton Goldsmith
EAN 978-1601630810

To Order Call 1-800-227-3371 or visit CareerPress.com